A HOMETOWN ALBUM
Cloquet's Centennial Story

> "He will triumph who understands how to conciliate and combine with the greatest skill the benefits of the past with the demands of the future.
> Joseph Nicolas Nicollet (1786-1843)

A HOMETOWN ALBUM
Cloquet's Centennial Story

Larry Luukkonen

Marlene Wisuri

 Carlton County Historical Society
Cloquet, Minnesota

FUNDING SPONSORS
The publication of this book has been made possible through the generosity of the following donors:

An Anonymous Donor

Marguerite and Russell Cowles in honor of Steve Joseph

Members Cooperative Credit Union

Bette Davis Moorman

Thrivent Financial for Lutherans

Wells Fargo Bank, Cloquet

Sappi Fine Papers of Cloquet donated the 60# Patina Matte Text
    and Aero Cover Stock paper for the printing of this volume.

Copyright © 2004 by Larry Luukkonen and Marlene Wisuri

All rights reserved. No part of this book may be reproduced in any form, except short excerpts for review and educational purposes, without the written permission of the publisher.

ISBN 0-9618959-7-7

Printed and bound in the United States of American by
Bang Printing, Brainerd, Minnesota
Book layout and design by Marlene Wisuri

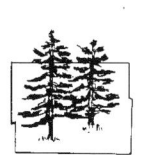

Carlton County Historical Society
406 Cloquet Avenue
Cloquet, MN 55720
218/879-1938
www.carltoncountyhs.org

COVER PHOTOGRAPHS:
    FRONT COVER ~
        Upper - Cloquet, looking east, 1881
        Lower - Pinehurst Park, c. 1909
        photos from the collection of the Carlton County Historical Society
    BACK COVER ~
        Upper - Cloquet Avenue, c. early 1940s
        Middle - Cloquet Avenue, c. 1950s
        photos from the collection of the Carlton County Historical Society
        Lower - Cloquet Avenue, 2003, photo by Allen Anway
                    used with permission

DEDICATION

This book is dedicated to the memory of people like Dan Cameron, Joseph Nahgahnub, George S. Shaw, Frederick and Rudolph Weyerhaeuser, John Bergeron, Henry Hornby, Swan Hawkinson, Anna Dickie and Peter Olesen, Joe Posey, Octavie Morneau, Olaf Olson, and many thousands more, who, each in their own special way, have contributed to the history of Cloquet.

ACKNOWLEDGEMENTS

We are grateful for the assistance of numerous people who helped with this publication. The Minnesota Historical Society provided a number of wonderful photographs. Special thanks go to Timothy J. Krohn who so generously shared his photographs taken for the Cloquet Centennial Committee, to Allen Anway for taking his view camera to the streets of Cloquet, and to Mike Sylvester of the *Pine Journal* for tracking down images for us. We extend appreciation to the many other people who provided photographs which have added greatly to the book. For help with the manuscript we are indebted to Karen Smith, Rod Boehlke, and Dan Naslund. We are also appreciative of Joseph Peterson's research on the mayors of Cloquet. Arnold Luukkonen provided identification for many photos and offered encouragement throughout the project. Roberta Malwitz and Harriette Niemi of the Carlton County Historical Society staff covered many hours while the layouts were being done, patiently proofread and offered advice, research help, and encouragement.

Our thanks to all of you.

The white pines at the Cloquet Foresty Center
c. early 1900s

ABOUT THE PHOTOS:

Unless otherwise indicated, all photographs are from the collection of the Carlton County Historical Society. All photographers are credited when known. Photos loaned to CCHS for this book are credited as such.

Minnesota Historical Society materials are used with permission.

This dramatic view shows a white pine log under the showers for its last bath at the Northern Lumber Company's mill.

Photo by Buckbee Mears Company, c. 1930, from the collection of the Minnesota Historical Society

CONTENTS

9   **Message from the Mayor**
by Mayor Bruce Ahlgren

11   **Publisher's Preface**
by Marlene Wisuri

12   **Introduction**
by Larry Luukkonen

15   **Chapter One**   The Crossroads

35   **Chapter Two**   The People

55   **Chapter Three**   Institutions and Organizations

77   **Chapter Four**   Village Life

99   **Chapter Five**   War, Disaster, and Depression

119   **Chapter Six**   A Resilient Community

137   **A Color Album**

153   **Bibliography**

156   **Suggested Reading**

157   **Index**

160   **About the Authors**

**Sylvester "Stokes" Wilson (1864-1927)
First Mayor of Cloquet**

Stokes Wilson came to Cloquet in 1883 and was employed as a machinist for the C. N. Nelson Lumber Company. He advanced to the position of chief engineer which he held until the fire of 1918. He married Josephine Bressette in Cloquet in 1890. They had three children and Stokes was active in civic affairs until the family left Cloquet after the fire. After moving out west for a time, the family returned to Duluth where Stokes died in July, 1927.

MAYORS OF THE CITY OF CLOQUET ~ 1904 - 2004

Stokes Wilson	December 1904 - 1910
C. I. McNair	1910 - 1912
William Kelly	1912 - 1914
Fred D. Vibert	1914 - 1915
Harry Dixon	1915 - 1918
John Long	1918 - 1920
J. E. Diesen	1920 - 1923
H. J. Hamann	1923 - 1924
J. J. Colburn	1924 - 1928
Fred C. Johnson	1928 - 1932
Harry Kaner	1932 - 1935
George W. DePoe	1936 - 1939
Roy W. Ranum	1940 - 1943
Carl J. Lind	1944 - 1947
Roy W. Ranum	1948 - 1953
Norman Halverson	1954 - 1957
Roy W. Ranum	1958 - 1966
Walter Stock	1966 - 1969
Dr. John T. McGregor	1970 - 1974
Floyd D. Jaros	1975 - 1976
Arlene Wolner	1976 - 1982
Mel Tan	1983 - 1988
Don Panger	1989 - 1944
Fred Little	1995 - 1998
Bruce Ahlgren	1999 - Present (2004)

Message From the Mayor of Cloquet

I am deeply honored to be Mayor of Cloquet during this centennial celebration. As a lifelong resident of Cloquet, I enjoy viewing the photographs that document the many changes that have taken place in my hometown over the past century. Although the population has remained relatively stable during the past thirty years, the city's boundaries have grown and many changes have taken place.

As you look at the photos of Cloquet that span the last one hundred years, think of the progress the people of this lumber town have made for Cloquet, past and present. Think of what the wood industries have done for our community by providing well-paying jobs for its citizens and stimulating many other businesses, as well as a much-needed hospital and a fine school system. Cloquet survived the 1918 fire, the Great Depression, world wars and other problems that have afflicted our city, county, state, and nation. Cloquet's record over the past one hundred years makes us proud of our community. Wherever we are in the world, we are never ashamed to say we hail from Cloquet, Minnesota.

Let your mind drift and think of the memories created in our small but industrious community. The Independence Day and Labor Day parades, complete with the Cloquet High School marching band and majorettes, the Shriners in their mini-cars, and the politicians; the yearly carnivals; the Veterans' Day salutes; the toot-toot of the trains as they rumble through town; the paper mill smell; the swimmers diving off "the rock" into the St. Louis River; the summertime baseball games scattered throughout the city; hockey, football, basketball, and the Pine Valley ski jumping meets are just a handful of the events that come to mind as I peer into my mind's eye of the past. There will be many more memories to be made in the century to come.

Welcome to Cloquet.

Bruce Ahlgren
Mayor of Cloquet

This early resident beckons us to stroll with her down the
wooden sidewalk into a century of Cloquet's history.

Publisher's Preface

As the Carlton County Historical Society celebrates the 55th anniversary of its founding in 2004, it seems entirely appropriate that we undertake the publication of a pictorial history of Cloquet, the largest city in Carlton County, during Cloquet's centennial year. This volume continues the Society's program of publishing local history that began with the publication of *Crossroads in Time: A History of Carlton County* by Dr. Francis Carroll in 1987. That first book was a leap of faith on the part of the Society's Board of Directors which was rewarded with a book critically recognized as among the finest examples of local history. The Society has continued its commitment to making Carlton County history available to the largest number of people through books. *A Hometown Album* becomes the sixth book of local history to be published by the Society since 1987.

It is a real pleasure to be able to use the fine photographic collection of the Society to tell Cloquet's centennial story. Photographs have the magical ability to jog our recollections and preserve memories that might otherwise be lost. The difficulty with a project such as this one is to make selections from the many possibilities. We wish we could have included much more and regret the omission of so many fine photos. We have attempted to include a representative sampling and hope that the personal albums of past and present Cloquet residents will help round out the story for individual readers.

My love of old photographs and the stories of the area is deep and abiding. Through the study of these relics we can learn much about our collective and personal history. It is our hope you will enjoy this look at Cloquet's last one hundred years in pictures and words.

Marlene Wisuri
Director, Carlton County Historical Society

It is not everyday that one celebrates a civic centennial. On such occasions it is tempting to look for a definitive history that can mark the passage of time by accurately portraying events or by showing certain important trends that helped to shape the growth of a community. There are a number of fine accounts that show important elements of Cloquet's history for part of the period from 1904 to 2004, but none offers a comprehensive history of the years in question. The purpose of this book is to bring the record up to date and define some of the major trends that influenced the community during its first century as a city.

Several important themes emerge from a study of the many works dealing with Cloquet's past. For example, the city's location at an ancient crossroads on the St. Louis River had a major impact on its future development. Furthermore, the interesting mixture of people who comprised the community, their social and cultural organizations, their ways of life, and the ways in which they dealt with a whole series of events that befell them, help to explain the origin of Cloquet and the events that shaped its unique character.

Actually, the first settlement near the present site of Cloquet goes back to the mid-1850s, almost fifty years before the city was organized in 1904. Then, in 1879, a boom company and a sawmill were established at what later became the village of Knife Falls. Drawn by the industrial potential of the waterpower of the Knife Falls, farsighted men saw the possibility of driving logs downstream and processing them into lumber. That first sawmill operation, located just above the Knife Falls where the St. Louis River makes a gradual bend to the north, eventually became the basis for a modern industrial center.

Almost from the beginning, the growth of the community was recorded in many ways, including official records, letters, maps, newspapers, and photographs. Interestingly enough, the progress of the town from a crude frontier settlement to a modern city occurred when the art of photography was being developed. Many aspects of Cloquet's history have been chronicled through the objective lenses of early cameras by photographers, both amateur and professional.

By combining the information contained in historical narratives and archival materials with the existing collection of photographs available at the Carlton County Historical Society, one can understand some of the factors that shaped the history of Cloquet. Through words and pictures one can travel back in time and see the steady rise of a frontier community into a respectable city. Hopefully, the reader will enjoy the story and perhaps profit from the experiences of those who created an enduring and resilient community.

Larry Luukkonen
Historian

A bird's-eye view of Cloquet in the early 1920s. The newly built city hall and Wentworth Square Park are visible in the foreground. The roof of the new depot can also be seen.

Fortress Island stands in the St. Louis River unaltered by time.
The top view shows the island as seen from the foot of Knife Portage.
The lower picture shows the pristine island set against a backdrop of industrial development.

Photos by Larry Luukkonen

Chapter One
The Crossroads

Long before there ever was a Cloquet there was a river that would determine the site of a city. The early French traders called it *La Rivière du Fond du Lac Supérieur* (The river at the end of Lake Superior); and, in the days when waterways were the highways of the wilderness, it was a major travel artery for anyone interested in penetrating the rugged country west of Lake Superior. We know it today as the St. Louis River. Cloquet's destiny was largely shaped by its location at a primitive crossroads, where a series of trails intersected the river.

The future site of Cloquet was located near the Knife Falls, at the beginning of the formidable Dalles of the St. Louis River. The water route was especially difficult for early travelers proceeding upstream. After negotiating the grueling nine-mile Grand Portage of the St. Louis, they would see Fortress Island signaling the beginning of the short but uncomfortable Knife Portage around the Knife Falls and a series of rapids.

After the travelers had completed the portage, they might have noticed the overland trails which crossed the time-honored canoe route above the Knife Falls. These trails were mostly used in winter for traveling over the swampy and uneven terrain. Known as "winter

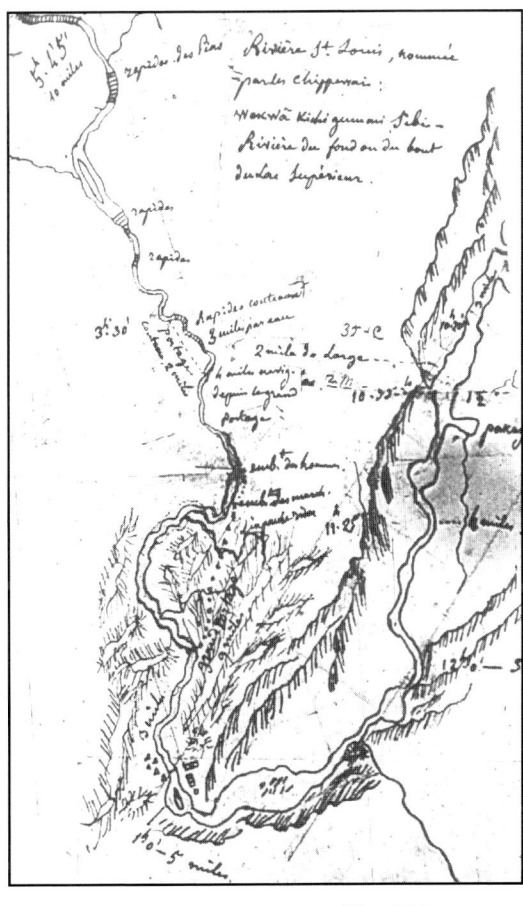

One of a series of detailed sketch maps of the St. Louis River, drawn in August of 1837, by the noted French explorer and mathematician Joseph N. Nicollet. The part reproduced here shows the St. Louis River and the future site of the city of Cloquet. Nicollet marked the distance by land and water as follows: *Rapids couteaux, 3 miles par eau, portage couteaux 2 miles.*

roads" to those familiar with the area, the trails were perhaps equally if not more important than the water route, for they were heavily used during winter, when travel overland by dog sled was faster and easier.

Not all early travel involved waterways. Probably just as much traffic moved over land in winter. Two common modes of travel in winter were by dog sled or on foot with snowshoes. This illustration, from Thomas L. McKenney's *Sketches of a Tour to the Lakes* (1827), shows the type of dog sled often used.

Long before the name *Cloquet* ever appeared on any map of the St. Louis River watershed, the term *Knife Falls* was commonly used to describe the waterfall at the beginning of roughly three miles of rapids that made the Knife Portage necessary. Known on many early maps as *Le Portage des Couteaux* (the carrying place of the knives), both the portage and the falls took their names from the upturned slate formation peculiar to the area. The sharp edges of the slate cut the soft wet moccasins worn by travelers and voyageurs, or boatmen, as they carried heavy loads of supplies and their canoes over the Knife Portage.

Travelers used the terms Knife Falls and Knife Portage many years before the name Cloquet appeared for the first time on a map drawn by Joseph N. Nicollet. Nicollet's map, published in 1843, named the Cloquet River, a major tributary of the St. Louis; and the Cloquet Rapids, located several miles north of the present city of Cloquet. Nicollet's use of the name Cloquet to describe both the river and the rapids was most likely the result of a corruption of the more common name *Cloutier*. An interesting story that supports this contention was recorded by a Methodist missionary in 1850.

The first mention of a settlement in the vicinity of the Knife Falls occurred shortly after the conclusion of a treaty with the Chippewa at La Pointe in 1854, which established the Fond du Lac Reservation immediately

A sketch of a type of snowshoe commonly used on the frontier, also from McKenney.

west of the future site of Cloquet. A small settlement composed of indigenous people, formerly residing near the old American Fur Company post in the village of Fond du Lac, was located along a ridge at a point where the St. Louis River gradually bends to the north. The village overlooked the Knife Falls and the junction of the overland trails near the Knife Portage. Shortly after the establishment of this village, the first wagon road in the area was built to haul supplies from the head of navigation at the village of Fond du Lac to the new village on the newly created reservation.

The village overlooking the St. Louis River was well-established when the official government survey of Knife Falls Township occurred in 1868. The official survey notes of the township, named for the prominent waterfall, recorded details of the trails, the village, the reservation, and the new Fond du Lac to Knife Falls wagon road. These first small beginnings on the banks of the St. Louis River went largely unnoticed for several years until commercial interest in the available water power and the

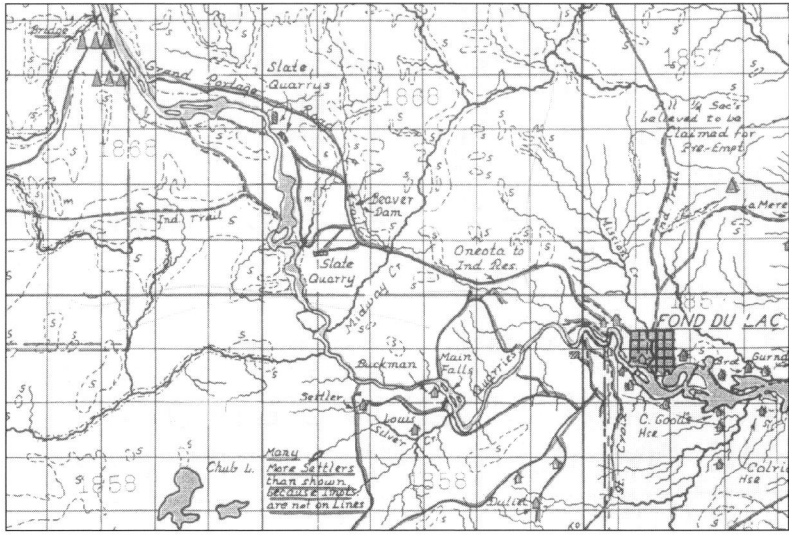

This composite map, based on an early United States Government Land Surveyor's field notes, shows several portages and overland trails near the future site of the city of Cloquet.

Map courtesy of J. W. Trygg Historic Collections

A sketch of the American Fur Company trading post at Fond du Lac in 1826, as seen from the St. Louis River. Following the conclusion of a treaty in 1854, the Fond du Lac band of Lake Superior Chippewa moved their village upstream to a bluff overlooking the future site of Cloquet. Later the Grand Portage wagon road was built to haul supplies from the head of navigation at Fond du Lac to the new village site.
Illustration from Thomas L. McKenney's *Sketches of a Tour to the Lakes*

potential for construction of a log boom on the St. Louis was recognized. It is significant, nonetheless, to note the earliest connection between the trade routes and the location of the first village near what would eventually become the city of Cloquet.

In 1879, the Knife Falls Boom Company built a log boom above the falls and the first sawmill was erected. A small settlement soon grew up around these commercial enterprises. In addition to the industrial development at the head of the falls, a railroad line was extended from Carlton, then called Northern Pacific Junction, to Knife Falls. From 1879 until 1883 the settlement near the sawmill was known only as Knife Falls. It was not until 1883 that the village was platted and subsequently renamed Cloquet.

In time, the railroad line, built by the St. Paul and Duluth Railroad to service Knife Falls, was extended farther up the valley of the St. Louis River and eventually connected with

This scene, reportedly taken along the St. Louis River in the 1870s, shows traditional birch bark wigwams and a canoe used by some of the inhabitants. The triangular white object located behind the woman in the center is a sail for a Mackinaw boat, a type of craft widely used on Lake Superior by early fur traders.

Photo by Charles A. Zimmerman from the collection of Minnesota Historical Society, c. 1870

The earliest known photograph of Cloquet taken on August 15, 1881. The small settlement shown here consisted of a dormitory and a number of frame houses clustered around a steam sawmill. A note written on the photograph states the dormitory burned in 1882.

lines serving the newly developed iron ore mines to the north. The Northern Pacific Railroad, begun at Carlton in 1870, built westward roughly paralleling the old trade routes along the St. Louis River and portions of the winter roads long used by traders traveling from the St. Louis River to the Mississippi, the Red River Valley, and beyond.

The railroads not only served to bring new settlers to the Cloquet area but, more importantly, also functioned as an efficient carrier for the timber products produced by the ever-increasing number of sawmills and related facilities being built there. The railroad also helped to bring logs to the mills. At first, loggers cut timber in remote areas and drove logs down various tributaries of the St. Louis River to Cloquet. Later, lumbermen realized greater efficiency by simply bringing the timber all the way to Cloquet by rail and dumping it into the river to await processing by the mills.

For decades following the establishment of the sawmilling industry at Cloquet, the role of the railroad seemed paramount. The portage paths and winter roads of the early travelers and traders were first supplemented by, and then finally replaced with, the railroad. Each mode of transportation built on the preceding type and each new form influenced in some way the growing settlement at Cloquet. By the beginning of the twentieth century a new system of transportation appeared which had a profound influence on the future development of the community.

Although early settlers built a number of wagon roads in the country around Cloquet during the nineteenth century, it was not until the twentieth century and the advent of cheap, mass-produced automobiles, that strong interest by local citizens in improving the road

Early inhabitants of the Indian village that preceded the settlement of Cloquet. Shown here are Mr. and Mrs. Joe Petite (seated) and Joe Posey (standing). Posey, for whom Posey Island is named, is said to have died under mysterious circumstances.

19

system brought needed change. Realizing the importance of a network of good roads, the state created a system of trunk highways designed to link key communities together independent of any other existing form of transportation.

The automobile provided individuals with a means to access more regions than any previous system of transportation. One can see its effect on Cloquet by noting the changing definition of "main street." One can also trace the process by noting the layout of the community and the ever-changing location of city hall.

In its formative years, Cloquet was platted facing the St. Louis River in what is today the western part of the city. Arch Street functioned as "main street" in the early days of the town. It was the gateway for anyone entering from the north. Later, as the city expanded, the focus shifted to Cloquet Avenue.

The main route through Cloquet from the north followed the state highway first across the "Red Bridge" to Dunlap Island, then across the "Iron Bridge" to the south side of the river and along Arch Street as far as Cloquet Avenue, then east along Cloquet Avenue. At Fourteenth Street, one abruptly turned south and continued along the state highway, commonly called the "Carlton Road," until it intersected with State Trunk Highway 2, otherwise known as the "Moorhead Road." The peculiar jog in Cloquet Avenue at the intersection with Fourteenth Street still amazes motorists.

As the highway system developed, other now familiar roads were constructed to connect Cloquet with surrounding communities. For example, State Highway 33 connected Trunk Highway 61 at Atkinson with Cloquet. Likewise, State Highway 45 linked Trunk Highway 61 at Scanlon with Cloquet Avenue at Fourteenth Street.

Following World War II, interest in providing Cloquet with a more direct connection to the junction of highways 61 and 210 led to the rerouting of old Highway 33.

> The official United States survey map of Knife Falls Township, made in 1868, shows roads, trails and portages. The survey notes indicate "The land in this township is very poor and wet." The surveyor also noted an "Indian village of 5 or 6 houses on the line at the top of river bluff."

In the process, part of Pinehurst Park was filled in and a large grove of virgin white pine south of the park that had escaped the forest fire in 1918 was cut and bulldozed to make way for the new highway. When completed, the new road provided travelers heading north with a direct route to Cloquet and the burgeoning cities on Minnesota's Iron Range. Subsequent construction of Interstate Highway 35 greatly enhanced Cloquet's position as the gateway to Northern Minnesota.

Throughout its history, Cloquet has benefitted by sitting astride main arteries of travel and commerce, be they rivers and portages, winter roads, railroads, or highways. Anyone who doubts the influence that modes of transportation have had over the years need only look in which direction the city is growing and continuing its role as a crossroads.

Reverend John B. Genin, O.M.I., served the Fond du Lac Reservation and the earliest inhabitants of Cloquet from 1873 to 1882.

A photograph, possibly dating to 1954, shows the congregation of Holy Family Mission. The location of the church building, overlooking the valley of the St. Louis River, is a reminder of the first successful settlement near the future site of Cloquet.

This plat map shows the village of Cloquet and Dunlap Island as being platted in 1882. Actually Dunlap Island was platted one year before Cloquet was officially platted. Featured prominently on the village map is the Knife Falls branch of the St. Paul & Duluth Railroad. The railroad provided a speedy and reliable means of transportation so lumber cut in Cloquet could reach markets throughout the Midwest.

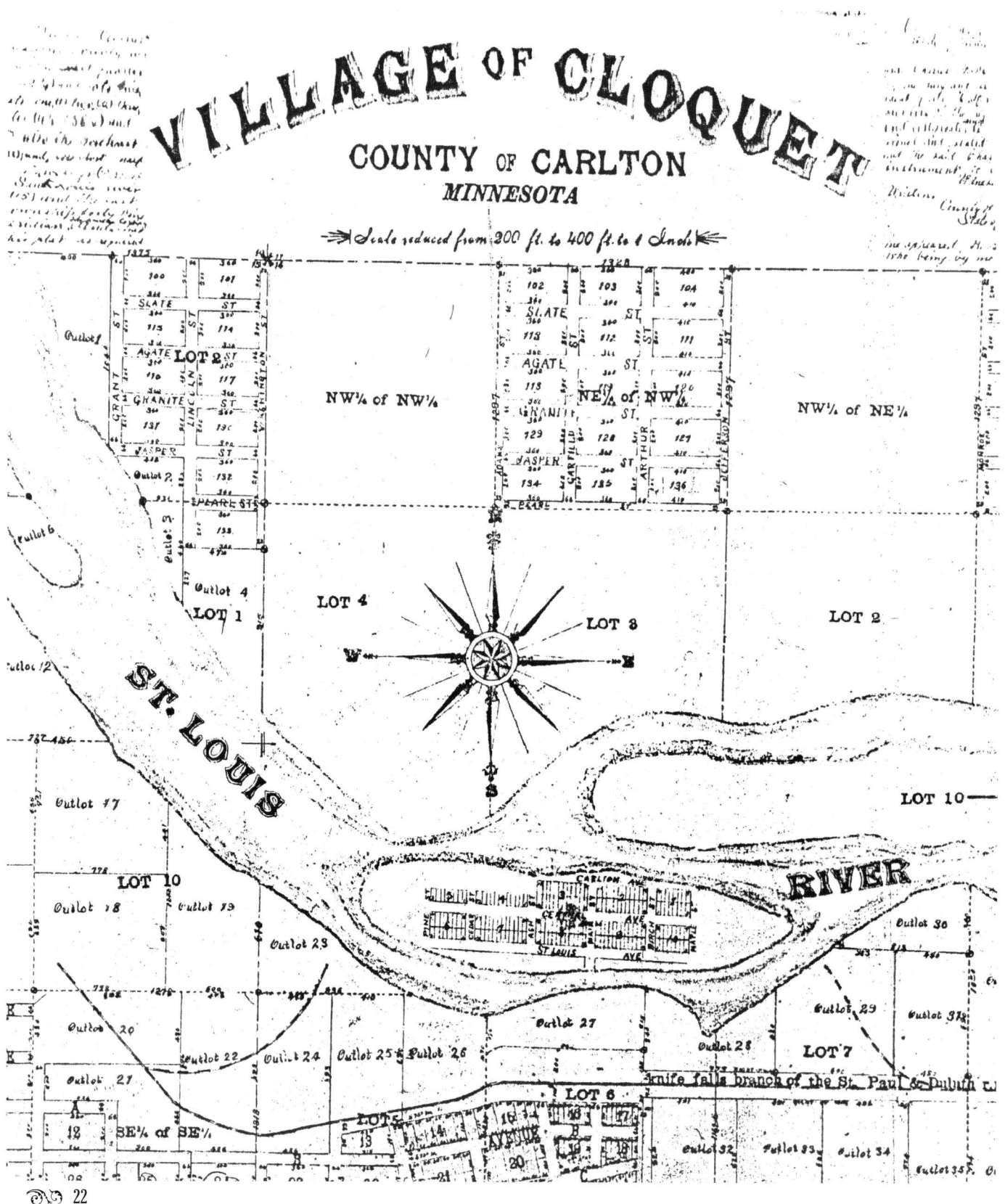

Large stands of virgin white pine in the St. Louis River watershed attracted the attention of logging companies. The logging operation recorded here was in Section 12 of Knife Falls Township near Cloquet. Most early logging took place in winter within easy hauling distance of major streams and employed horses and oxen for skidding the large loads of timber.

Waterways were vital to the economical movement of logs to the sawmills. Logging dams were built to ensure a plentiful supply of water to float the logs downstream. The Knife Falls Dam shown here was typical of the timber and stone crib dams constructed along the St. Louis River and other major rivers. The first opening on the left side of the dam was the sluice way where logs could be passed through to sawmills below. The Knife Falls Dam also provided sufficient water for a mill pond to serve mills located upstream.

Photo by Roy Keizer from the collection of the Minnesota Historical Society, c. 1910

A typical example of the method employed for moving saw logs from the woods to nearby streams. The load of logs shown here seems too big for the team of horses to move, but the sleigh was pulled along ice roads which greatly reduced friction.

Photo from the collection of the Minnesota Historical Society, 1907-08

Logs awaiting processing at the Cloquet Lumber Company's sawmill.
Scenes such as this were commonplace during the era of the large steam sawmills.
Photo by Buckbee Mears Co. from the collection of the Minnesota Historical Society, c. 1930

A fine early view of Cloquet and two of the five sawmills which established the village as a major lumber production center. In the foreground one sees the village with its rows of wooden houses. In the center, the Northern Lumber Company lower sawmill dominates the river front. In the upper left corner is the upper Northern mill. Stretching into the distance are the booms which held each individual sawmill's logs. The diagonal line crossing the river in the distance is the Posey Island railroad bridge.

Construction of the Great Northern Railroad in Cloquet. Note the narrow-gauge tramway used to remove construction debris and excavated material from the right of way. The Great Northern Railroad extended northwest up the St. Louis River Valley and on into the western states. A considerable amount of lumber processed in Cloquet was sent by rail to help build new homes and towns in the far west.

In 1924 the last log drive to Cloquet on the St. Louis River was completed. After that time, most logs destined for the sawmills were hauled by rail and dumped into the river to await processing. Trains, such as the one shown here operated by the Duluth & Northeastern Railroad (D&NE) Company, were a common sight. The use of railroads for logging not only extended the area that could be logged, but also made log transportation a year-round business.

Railroad logging was faster than using river routes, but it could also be more dangerous. On March 17, 1917, D&NE Engine Number 16 jumped the tracks on the Dunlap Island side of the St. Louis River railroad bridge and plunged through the ice. The engineer and fireman escaped unhurt, but the brakeman riding in the cab was killed. This photograph shows Number 16 being pulled from the river by a huge steam crane. It is reported that the bridge had to be strengthened to accommodate the extra weight of both pieces of equipment.

Photo courtesy of Dick Brenner

A view of the Northern Lumber Company's mills at Cloquet before 1918. The Northern Lumber Company operated two mills at that time. They were referred to as the "Upper Northern" and the "Lower Northern." In the foreground is the company's planing mill with box cars waiting to be loaded with finished product. In the background is the upper Northern sawmill and seemingly endless stacks of lumber drying in the sun.

A view of the busy loading dock at the Cloquet Lumber Company. Note lumber is being shipped in both standard open cars and in box cars. All of the five sawmills that operated in Cloquet had shipping facilities in addition to processing operations.

Photo from the collection of the Minnesota Historical Society, c. 1930

With the advent of motor transportation, railroad logging operations conducted by the D&NE were gradually phased out. Trucks could reach more remote locations quicker and with less expense than the railroads. The twilight of the era of logging railroads came in the 1960s, the same time that steam locomotives were being replaced with diesel. Shown here is Engine Number 28, one of the last steam locomotives used on the D&NE, pulling three passenger cars and its distinctive caboose during a special tour from Cloquet to Saginaw in the 1960s.

For most citizens in early Cloquet, the horse provided the means of transportation around town and the surrounding countryside. The netting worn by the horse shown in the photograph was intended to protect the animal from horse flies and other biting insects.

Large numbers of horses were used by the logging companies and local sawmills in addition to those employed by residents or neighborhood businesses. Livery stables were a common sight in every town. Individuals could rent a horse and wagon or obtain supplies and feed for the animal. The livery stable shown here was located near the intersection of Avenue C and Arch Street.

If one did not own a horse, other animals could be used in a pinch. Here, young Fritz Anderson has hitched his pet sheep to a sled. A similar method of using horses to pull large sleighs was employed by fur traders who operated in Northern Minnesota. References to "horse trains" can be found in early correspondence.

Photo courtesy of Jody Acers

By the early twentieth century, another popular means of local transportation was the bicycle. This photograph, by Octavie Morneau, shows two intrepid cyclists posing with their machines.

By the 1920s improved roads and the development of a state trunk highway system, made the automobile the common means of year-round transportation. The photograph shown here is a typical country road near Cloquet in the 1930s.

The automobile repair garage became the successor to the livery stable. Shown here is the interior of McCoy and Sapp's Garage with the service crew posing in front of vintage automobiles.

For those who did not own an automobile early bus service provided an inexpensive means of travel. Scheduled service between Cloquet and Duluth was provided by the Cloquet-Duluth Transit Company bus, shown here on a Duluth street in the 1910s.

HEY! HEY!
The New Fleet Is COMING!
Watch For the Big Parade of
HEBERT'S
—NEW—
DODGE TAXI'S
100 FREE 100
RIDES
Ride in Comfort, Class, Safety and the Latest in Streamline
712 712
For SERVICE For SAFETY

Another alternative means of transportation for those wishing to travel in the Cloquet area was the Hebert Taxi service begun by Walter E. "Spec" Hebert in the 1930s. By the 1940s, Cloquet boasted a taxi fleet and drivers as shown here.

By the 1940s, individual motorists could have their vehicles serviced or purchase repair parts at places like the Cloquet Auto & Supply Company. Note the vine covered canopy and gasoline dispensers on the curb.

The appearance of the Cloquet Auto & Supply Company building was altered as part of the ever-changing face of main street. The canopy is gone, but the curbside gasoline pumps are apparently still providing handy service for passing motorists.

31

Two views of "main street." The first photograph shows Arch Street at Ave C before the Fire of 1918. Note the delivery wagon and horse in the background. The local denizens in the foreground are keenly aware that they are about to be captured on film for posterity. The lower photograph shows Cloquet Avenue at Eighth Street. The paved street, sidewalks, street lighting, signs, and heavy traffic stand in sharp contrast to the earlier street scene.

Over the years, Cloquet has had four city halls. The reason for this is due in part to the ever-changing face of main street as much as any other factor. Business and traffic patterns were constantly changing and buildings changed to reflect these realities. The first city hall was a two story brick structure located near the heart of the business district. The city hall was completely destroyed in the Fire of 1918.

Cloquet's second city hall was a substantial brick and concrete structure surmounted by an imposing federal eagle. It was located facing Arch Street, then the major thoroughfare through town.

Photo from the collection of the Minnesota Historical Society, c. 1920

In the 1960s, both the city hall and the Cloquet Fire Department were relocated to the former YMCA building on Cloquet Avenue between Fourth and Fifth streets. The Cloquet Police Department was later relocated to the same site. Subsequent alterations were made to the building in an effort to make it suitable as a government and emergency services center, but neither goal was accomplished.

In the spring of 1990 work began on the fourth city hall located at the corner of Fourteenth Street and Cloquet Avenue.

Good to the last drop! In a scene reminiscent of a Norman Rockwell painting, a group of children savor the flavors of the Cloquet Bridgeman's ice cream store sometime during the 1960s.

Photograph courtesy of Robert Minogue

Chapter Two

The People

It seems as though someone has always lived near the Knife Falls. Maybe it was only a temporary encampment, perhaps a seasonal shelter or even a crude cabin, but since the earliest time, travelers have occasionally noted the presence of someone in the vicinity of the falls. The first documented reference of someone staying at the falls dates to 1784. In the fall of that year, fur trader Jean Baptiste Perrault camped near *Le Portage des Couteaux* for a time. His journal contains the first specific written reference to the place.

Among the earliest residents of the Cloquet area was Chief Joseph Nahgahnub (also spelled Nagonub). Note the elaborately carved pipe he is holding. His "Chief's Coat" appears to be patterned after an early nineteenth century style military coat.

Photo by William McLeish from the collection of the Minnesota Historical Society, c. 1880

Since Perrault's time, others have remarked about persons living nearby. Whether it was a camp of indigenous people or a sawmill hand's crude cabin, this location situated at a frontier crossroads appears to have been a natural place to congregate. Who were these people who were drawn to the banks of the St. Louis River?

Already mentioned is the presence of indigenous people near the future site of the city of Cloquet. Venerable family names such as Beargrease, Nahgahnub, Northrup, and Whitebird, to mention a few, still survive to this day. They were joined by the scions of old French-Canadian families. Names such as Dufault, LeGarde, Landrie, Morrisette, Roussain or Roy are found on the rosters of clerks and voyageurs who once worked for the old North West Company of Montreal or John Jacob Astor's American Fur Company. Many of these men intermarried with local families.

Two unidentified elders from the Fond du Lac Reservation posed for Cloquet photographer Octavie Morneau around 1910.

Added to the collection of names were several English and Scottish families such as Durfee, Morrison, McDonald, and McGillis, also known to have worked for the great fur companies. Descendants of these families were found at Cloquet when the area began to be developed for timber production in the last quarter of the nineteenth century.

In addition to the families who had roots in the area, new names of workers associated with the building of the railroads began to appear. Many recent Irish and German immigrants worked as laborers on the construction gangs assigned to build the Northern Pacific Railroad, the Lake Superior and Mississippi Railroad, and other railroads in the 1870s and early 1880s. Some undoubtedly stayed in the area, and their names are to be found on the first federal census taken of the future city of Cloquet.

Photographers, such as Olaf Olson and Octavie Morneau, took many photographs of people and places in Cloquet during the opening years of the twentieth century. Their work captured the essential spirit of the community for posterity.

Born in St. Jean Port Joli, Quebec, Octavie Morneau arrived in Cloquet in 1901 at the age of 34, and soon opened a photography studio on Arch Street. The Morneau Art Studio produced hundreds of portraits, group pictures, industrial views, logging scenes, and photo novelties.

Olaf Olson, a Norwegian immigrant, had lived in Cloquet for sixteen years when he opened his portrait studio in 1907. He had been trained at the Illinois College of Photography and later made some of the most memorable views of Cloquet following the fire of 1918.

Among those who eventually settled in what would become Cloquet were not only immigrant railroad workers, but more recent immigrants from the Scandinavian countries. Also present were seasoned lumberjacks from the wilds of Maine and New Brunswick who were following the logging frontier west. The mixture of native languages must have made for many a colorful conversation as the newcomers tried to make themselves understood through a thick brogue.

Newly arrived immigrants tended to stick together, and those who settled in early Cloquet were no exception. Names were given to neighborhoods populated by specific groups, and references to such exotic localities as "Little Canada" or "Finn town" sprinkled the everyday speech of local residents. Some workers built their homes near their places of employment, and references to areas such as "Shaw Town," "Nelson Town," or "Johnson Town" were common, since the residents of these neighborhoods tended to strongly identify with the sawmills that employed them.

Traditionally, some histories have focused exclusively on the careers of leading businessmen, politicians, or entrepreneurs while attempting to tell a comprehensive story of the founding of a particular community. While it is true that it took men of vision and those willing to take a chance to build many frontier communities, it was also true that countless workers, great and small, translated those visionaries' dreams into reality. In this respect, Cloquet was no different from other burgeoning towns on the edge of civilization. Lumberjacks, mill workers, farmers, and small businessmen, along with professionals such as educators, physicians, and attorneys all had a hand in creating the history of the community. It is a process that continues today.

Daniel Cameron, shown here late in life, was one of the first timber cruisers employed in Northern Minnesota and also one of Cloquet's earliest residents, coming to the village site in 1873. Dan Cameron died in Cloquet in 1944 at the age of 99.

By the 1870s new settlers began to arrive in the Cloquet area. These new residents, chiefly drawn from the ranks of lumberjacks and railroad employees, opted to settle in the community probably because it was close to their work and offered them necessary conveniences and services.

Photo by C. N. Johnson Studio of Cloquet

To be sure, Cloquet had its share of visionaries and entrepreneurs who were responsible for building the businesses that helped to attract people to the site of the future city. Among the first were James Smith, Jr., Dwight M. Sabin, William R. Merriam, and C. H. Graves, who organized the Knife Falls Boom Company to sort logs cut upstream on the St. Louis River watershed. The company began operations in 1879, the date generally assigned to the founding of Cloquet.

In that same year, a branch line of the St. Paul and Duluth Railroad was extended from Carlton to Knife Falls, and the first steam sawmill, later known as the Knife Falls Lumber Company, was established by Sheldon H. Olds, Henry Brandenburg, and William D. Harwood. It was the first of five sawmills built at Cloquet. In 1880 another sawmill was constructed upstream from Dunlap Island by Charles N. Nelson. He moved a second mill from Stillwater to Cloquet in 1889, thus making his operation the largest in Cloquet for a time.

Two other sawmills were started in Cloquet. In 1882, James M. Paine and William McNair built the Water Power Company mill. It was so named because it derived part of its power directly from the river by use of

Early settlement in Cloquet tended to cluster around the big steam sawmills, such as the Cloquet Lumber Company (formerly the Knife Falls Lumber Company) seen here. Although the sawmills appear similar at first glance, their distinctive design, smoke stacks, and refuse burners make them easily identifiable.

a turbine. The balance of the mill machinery, however, was run by steam.

In 1884 a group of lumbermen headed by Frederick Weyerhaeuser and George S. Shaw, bought the Knife Falls Lumber Company. In 1886 it was renamed the Cloquet Lumber Company, possibly in keeping with the name given to the newly organized (1884) village of Cloquet. The choice of the name "Cloquet" for the mill and the town is not surprising, given that much of the timber processed by the sawmills originated in the Cloquet River Valley. In 1889 Shaw also purchased the Water Power Company, thus adding to the production capacity of the Cloquet Lumber Company.

The last of the five sawmills built in Cloquet was the Johnson-Wentworth mill, constructed in 1894, by Samuel S. Johnson. The new mill, constructed east of the Water Power Company, had a greater production capacity than any other Cloquet mill.

Men working the "hot pond" at the Northern Lumber Company's lower mill located on the site of the U.S. Gypsum plant's boiler room. The man in the white shirt is poling logs toward the "jack ladder" which hauled them up an incline into the upper story of the mill for processing. One can see the logs receiving their last bath before disappearing into the mill.

Photo from the collection of the Minnesota Historical Society

Other names of business entrepreneurs appearing after this time in connection with the establishment of the Northwest Paper Company in 1898 were Frederick Weyerhaeuser (and sons Charles A., Rudolph M., and Frederick E.), Drew Musser, and C. I. McNair. Two years later, Weyerhaeuser interests established the Cloquet Tie and Post Company to harvest cedar and tamarack from company lands.

Other wood products companies founded in Cloquet included the Cloquet Box Company, established in 1904 (later known as the Rathbone-Hair-Ridgway Company); the Berst-Forster-Dixfield Company, created in 1905; and the Diamond Match Company, which operated a match block factory in Cloquet from 1905 to 1908. Historians have pointed out that from 1880 to 1910 Cloquet was a major wood products center. This is not surprising given the production figures for the amount of lumber and other forest products manufactured during those years. But what of the countless men and women who worked to achieve the annual profits the industry posted?

It took skills of many sorts to wrest a living from the forests that surrounded Cloquet. One such skill was the art of estimating the volume of standing timber, otherwise known as "timber cruising." Working alone in the forests estimating the pine stumpage on "40s" and "80s," timber cruisers like Dan Cameron and Percy Vibert contributed to the handsome profits made by the companies. Lumber companies would build railroad spurs, construct logging camps, and assign crews of men to cut the pine, all based on the report of the timber cruiser.

Railroad workers, such as the Northern Pacific section crew shown here on a handcar, frequently settled close to their place of employment.

Photo courtesy of JoAnn Harden

Three employees of the Johnson-Wentworth Lumber Company about 1915. The men (shown left to right) are Charles Crider, A. McKale, and Frank Newman. All three men are shown wearing old suit pants and vests, which was common since the men needed pockets and shirts had only one. The men may be foremen since each has a notebook and pencils in his breast pocket.

Photo from the collection of the Minnesota Historical Society

While the timber cruisers worked alone to estimate the available timber, other specialized wood workers also contributed to the value of the product by applying their skills in felling trees and cutting them into the most advantageous lengths to maximize profits. Such was the skill of these men in locating, cutting, transporting, and sawing the timber that each in turn added value to the forest products harvested.

Skilled mill workers also had a hand in adding value to the products brought from the forest. Highly specialized men such as millwrights kept the machines in peak operating efficiency. Lumber graders could tell at a glance the value of a board as it came rushing down the sorting platform toward them. Skilled sawyers could look at a log and tell how best to position it on the saw carriage. By a system of hand signals called "deaf and dumb," the sawyer communicated with the carriage operator over the deafening whine of the saws to turn the log until his practiced eye determined the best cut. So skillful were the sawyers in the use of "deaf and dumb" that they not only gave split-second instructions to the carriage operator but also could cast doubt on his legitimacy if he misinterpreted those instructions.

Millwrights kept the sawmills humming. This photograph of a group of five millwrights was taken around 1905 at the Brooks-Scanlon sawmill in nearby Scanlon. The man standing second from the left holding a wrench is Swan Hawkinson. Swan, a Swedish immigrant who first came to Cloquet in 1882, worked not only at the Brooks-Scanlon Lumber Company, but also at the Northern Lumber Company's upper mill, and finally for the Wood Conversion Company. Like most sawmill hands, he worked in the logging camps in winter and in the sawmills in summer. During his working career, Swan made the transition from working with timber to working with wood fiber products.

Of course there were many other workers whose skills, trades, or crafts contributed to the life and growth of Cloquet. In more recent times we have seen the growth of industries and services that have no connection whatsoever to the forest industry, yet there is still a strong identification with the persona of the lumberjack. From its earliest beginning as a commercial city to the present day, Cloquet has retained the aura of a "sawdust city." Businesses, sports teams, and social organizations have frequently turned to the image of the lumberjack for a name or logo.

Today each ethnic group in the city claims part of the heritage of the lumberjack largely because some family member worked in the forest industry. The era of the large steam sawmills ended by the 1930s, but the image of the lumberjack lives on. Cloquet's population has become ever more diverse, largely because of a changing economy, improved transportation, and communication. New manufacturing and service industries have also attracted new inhabitants. Regardless of these new advances, the image of the lumberjack and of the glory days of the sawmill industry survives in the minds of the residents. Whether or not one's ancestors were numbered among the earliest inhabitants, there is a certain continuity in the shared heritage all have with the lumberjack. Perhaps this continuity is what attracts people to the banks of the St. Louis River and the place called Cloquet.

Among the many faces associated with the history of Cloquet were men and women who made the sawmills run and the community flourish. One such individual was John Bergeron, Pond Foreman for the Cloquet Lumber Company. Mr. Bergeron was also a well-known birler who could seemingly walk on water with his calk boots. Shown here around 1920, Bergeron is walking on floating logs in the booms between the Duluth & Northeastern Railroad bridge on Dunlap Island and the Northern Lumber Company's lower mill.

Photo from the collection of the Minnesota Historical Society

A group of workmen at the Johnson-Wentworth Lumber company posing for the camera. The group in front is seated on one of the many tram cars used to carry lumber from the mill to the drying yards. The crew includes foremen, oilers, sawyers, millwrights, lumber graders, and ordinary mill hands. Each person, no matter what his job, had a part to play in making the mills profitable.

Of all the many faces associated with the history of Cloquet, none is perhaps as familiar as that of George Stearns Shaw. He was a central figure at the very beginning of Cloquet's development as a sawmill center. This picture of Shaw, who died in 1897, was prominently featured in an article in the *American Lumberman* magazine in 1905.

Frederick's son, Rudolph Weyerhaeuser, managed the Northern Lumber Company (formerly the C.N. Nelson Lumber Company) mills in Cloquet. He was also instrumental in the formation of the Northwest Paper Company in 1898, and served as the first president of the new company.

Frederick Weyerhaeuser's name is synonymous with the American lumber industry. His various business decisions eventually shaped the destiny of Cloquet. Mr. Weyerhaeuser, pictured here, appears to have had as good an eye for ripe fruit trees as he had for quality timber.

Mr. L.F. Leach, shown seated in his office at the Johnson-Wentworth Lumber Company about 1925, was not only active in the forest products business, but also in civic affairs. He was elected Third Ward Alderman in 1904 when Cloquet reorganized as a city. His business office was typical of the time. Note the nickel-plated telephone on the roll-top desk. The room behind Leach was apparently used by clerks and draftsmen as indicated by the furniture.

Photo from the collection of the Minnesota Historical Society

Mr. William K. McNair was another businessman closely associated with Cloquet's forest industry. He is shown here in an early family portrait with his wife, Mary, and children, John, Ann, and William taken shortly after the turn of the twentieth century.

Henry Crook Hornby literally grew up with the timber industry in Cloquet. His first job was as a timekeeper for Renwick, Shaw & Crosset (later the Knife Falls Lumber Company and subsequently the Cloquet Lumber company). In 1906, he became the manager of the Cloquet Lumber Company. Hornby was keenly interested in the economic future of Cloquet.

In pre-fire Cloquet, the majority of homes, such as the one shown here, were modest dwellings. The proud couple and their two children stand in front of a chicken wire and board enclosure that may have contained a garden. Note the rain barrels on the side of the house. Rainwater was not only used to water plants, but also many women believed it beneficial for washing their hair.

The large two-story house shown here, with its stained glass windows and gingerbread decoration, belonged to Ed Monroe, the brother of photographer Octavie Morneau. No rain barrels are visible here. Instead, gutters and downspouts carry water away from the foundation. While some decorative shrubbery is evident, it does not appear that the owner maintained a garden.

This substantial brick house with trees, shrubs, and manicured lawn probably belonged to a mill owner or other person of means. Large homes, such as this, were indicative of a person's wealth and social status. They were expensive to build, required more maintenance, and tended to be built only in certain neighborhoods.

45

The various ethnic groups which settled in and around Cloquet identified strongly with certain churches and social organizations.

Pictured here, in a photograph from 1906, are the members of the Daughters of Norway.

The confirmation class of 1928 at St. Casimir's Church, located at Tenth Street and Carlton Avenue, posed on the front steps of the church.

St. Casimir's Catholic Church was known as the "Polish Church." The congregation merged with Our Lady of the Sacred Heart, the "French Church," to form the Queen of Peace Parish in 1994.

Of course, numerous people have been married in Cloquet over the years. These photos captured the changes in wedding styles as they recorded the weddings of a few Cloquet couples.

Left to right: August Norman and Annie Ullman were married in Cloquet on October 17, 1903.

Mike and Maggie Smith were wed July 17, 1917. (Photo from the collection of the Minnesota Historical Society)

Estelle and Oliver Huot said their vows on October 10, 1924.

Children were often prepared for their adult roles through such activities as this "mock" kindergarten wedding which took place on February 23, 1939.

Mary Dormanen and Francis W. Tuominen are surrounded on their wedding day in November, 1963, by their Cloquet High School classmates of that year.

47

Dr. T. Schantz-Hanson, most widely known for his work as Director of the University of Minnesota's Cloquet Forest Experimental Station, was also the first president of the Carlton County Historical Society founded in 1949. Dr. Schantz-Hanson is shown here around 1930 with G.E. Marshall of the Northwest Paper Company discussing the use of auxiliary forests. The "Experimental Station," as it was commonly called, is "the oldest experimental forest under continuous management by a university in the United States."

Photos left and below (by Chambers Studio) from the collection of the Minnesota Historical Society

Peter's wife, Anna Dickie Olesen, shown here in a photograph dating from 1920, was interested in Cloquet's educational system and also active in civic affairs and politics. In 1922 she was the first woman to be nominated by a major political party (Democratic) for a United States Senate seat. She lost the election, but made history. Locally, she is perhaps best known for her work during the Franklin Roosevelt administration to obtain the remainder of relief money promised fire victims by the federal government.

Peter Olesen was hired as Cloquet's Superintendent of Schools in 1909. Olesen had ambitious plans for the district including the construction of a $100,000 High School. The brand new building was completed shortly before the disastrous Fire of 1918. The ruined school was replaced by 1921. Two new elementary schools were also built, L.F. Leach School in 1919 and Jefferson School in 1923.

Of the many attorneys who have provided necessary legal services for the citizens of Cloquet, only one from the community has ever served on the Minnesota Supreme Court. Associate Justice Lawrence Yetka is shown here in his judical robes.

Photo courtesy Minnesota Court Information Office.

Famous for his detailed knowledge of early loggers in Minnesota, longtime Cloquet resident J.C. "Buzz" Ryan is shown feeding deer at the Cloquet Valley Ranger station in the 1960s. Born in Bemidji, Ryan moved to Cloquet in 1922 to work on fire claims. In 1929 he was employed by the State of Minnesota and he worked as a District Ranger and Forester until his retirement on October 3, 1970.

Photo from the collection of the Minnesota Historical Society

From the very beginning of the community, the people of Cloquet have had the services of a number of fine physicians. Shown here are two generations of family physicians who have made Cloquet their home. From left to right, doctors Ricard Puumala, Barbara Meyer Puumala, Marie Bepko Puumala, and Reino H. Puumala.

Cloquet was also known as the home of well-known movie stars. Oscar winning actress, Jessica Lange, shown in a photograph taken in 1982, graduated from Cloquet High School in 1967 and has starred in numerous motion pictures. She also serves as a special UNICEF Goodwill Ambassador and has paricipated in missions to Africa.

Photo © Columbia Pictures Industries, used with permission

Barbara Peyton was another popular movie actress from Cloquet. She is pictured here with actor Gregory Peck in the historical action melodrama *Only the Valiant.* c. 1950

Many noted celebrities have visited Cloquet over the years including Gloria Hall, noted aviatrix. This photograph, taken in 1932, shows Mayor Harry Kaner greeting Ms. Hall in front of city hall during her barnstorming tour in the area.

Less well-known, but perhaps just as famous in their own way, was the Garfield School "Kitchen Band." Members of this interesting ensemble posed for this 1939 photograph complete with homemade instruments and uniforms. The women appear ready to burst into some popular melody of the time.

Photo by Olaf Olson courtesy of JoAnn Harden

Summertime can be a time to enjoy the many opportunities for recreation in the region. In this 1960s photograph, a group of boy scouts and leaders from Scout Troop 174, are about to embark on an adventure-filled canoe trip.

Photo courtesy of George Hudler

51

Life for most residents throughout Cloquet's history was rather tranquil as suggested by this 1916 photograph. Elizabeth Coy and her brother Edward D. Coy are playing on the new concrete sidewalks along a tree-lined residential street.

This 1939 Christmas display made by the Cloquet Fire Department featured a peaceful street scene with figures, cars, and street lighting strangely reminiscent of the old lighting on Cloquet Avenue. Perhaps this is how the majority of residents saw their town and country, even as the rest of the world was plunged into a long and bloody war in Europe and Asia.

Photo by Olaf Olson

In 1950, the "West End Gang" found Cloquet to be a great place for the adventures of childhood.

Left to right: Bruce Swanson, Tom Canfield, Dale Manley, Dave Jenkins, Stuart Copeland, George Maki, Jim Christenson, and Chuck Noble.

Photo courtesy of Jerry Canfield

Throughout the history of Cloquet many faces have been captured on film, but this artist's image of two lumberjacks birling, while a Northwest Mounted Policeman watches from a logger's bateau, was the picture chosen for the cover of Cloquet's 1948 "Sawmill Days" celebration.

The image of the lumberjack was faithfully captured by this jolly crew clad in woolen clothing for the 1948 "Sawmill Days" celebration. Note the assortment of axes, pike poles, saws, and log scales brandished by this eager bunch. They were by all indications ready for action in the woods.

Smile! Klippen Scandinavian Lodge #3 members pose for a formal portrait in this early twentieth century photograph. Although most of the names of the members are unknown, it is evident organizations like the one pictured played an important role in the community.

Chapter Three
Institutions and Organizations

Many people have comprised the population of Cloquet since it was founded. Some were instrumental in developing various civic institutions or organizations. Several of these groups were religious, others social, and some political. Collectively, their stories narrate the changing lifestyle of the inhabitants, the times, and the important activities of ordinary people throughout the history of Cloquet.

Of all the institutions ever founded in Cloquet, schools must be seen as one of the most important. From the schools flowed the creative talent essential to all other activities that made the life of the community meaningful and productive. Education, in some form, existed in the region from the earliest time. For example, indigenous people not only had a social structure and religious institutions, but also a method of education through oral traditions passed down from one generation to the next.

In the 1830s, however, a new development occurred that had a profound impact, not only on indigenous peoples, but also on the future community. The beginning of missionary activity in Northern Minnesota at such places as Sandy Lake, Fond du Lac, Leech Lake, and other early

The Holy Family Mission Church was built about 1889 at the Indian settlement near the St. Louis River. The congregation and visiting priests are pictured in this photo taken by Octavie Morneau about 1910.

trade centers, introduced not only Christianity to the local population, but also reading and writing.

The missionaries believed that before the population could receive the basic tenets of the faith, they must first be able to read the scriptures and express themselves orally and in writing. Thus these first missions functioned as the first schools in the region.

Cloquet has a number of unique church buildings. Pictured here is the interior of Our Lady of the Sacred Heart Church after it was rebuilt following the Fire of 1918. Note the graceful Roman colonnades typical of Italian Renaissance churches.

The churches and schools of Cloquet had their roots in the early missionary activities of the Congregationalists, Methodists, Presbyterians, and Roman Catholics, along with others. They were responsible for spreading the faith and the art of communication. In fact, Cloquet boasted several churches along with schools during the development of the village.

Members of the 1903 Norwegian Lutheran confirmation class, dressed in their best finery, hold their graduation certificates for all to see.

The first church actually built in Cloquet was the Roman Catholic Church of the Holy Names of Jesus and Mary in 1882. Twenty years later the congregation had grown so much that a new facility was needed. Accordingly, a larger church, Our Lady of the Sacred Heart, was built on Avenue F and Fifth Street. Four years later a new school was added on the south side of that building to serve the growing educational needs of the church community. Meanwhile, the spiritual needs of the growing Polish community in Cloquet were met with the construction of St. Casimir's Catholic Church in 1910.

The first Protestant church built in Cloquet was the Presbyterian Church of Cloquet, formed in 1883. It also grew rapidly and, by 1916, boasted a new brick building at the intersection of Fourth Street and Avenue F. It was soon followed by other denominations. In 1893, the congregation of what would later become St. Andrew's Episcopal Church was formed. Part of the growing Scandinavian element in Cloquet's population was represented by the new Swedish Evangelical Lutheran Church completed in 1886.

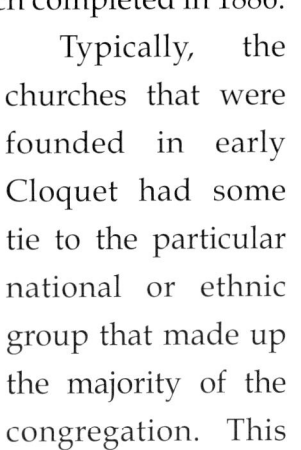

The Presbyterian Church of Cloquet shortly after it was rebuilt following the Fire of 1918. Note the city water tank in the background and the desolate appearance of the hillside. The small object which appears to be hanging in the air in front of the church is actually an arc light, a type of early street light.

Photo by H. W. Sable

Typically, the churches that were founded in early Cloquet had some tie to the particular national or ethnic group that made up the majority of the congregation. This trend was reflected not only in the various Scandinavian churches but in other organizations as well. Pride in one's national origin and interest in one's native culture were indicative of the strong sense of nationalism prevalent then.

Church membership was important to many residents of Cloquet as indicated by this photograph, taken in the early 1920s. The congregation of St. Paul's Church, located at the corner of Tenth Street and Avenue F, was mainly Finnish-American.

Not only did the early churches in Cloquet provide religious services and instruction, but several also offered a regular school curriculum, thus providing an important addition to Cloquet's educational system. Some, such as the Swedish Evangelical Lutheran Church, helped to preserve elements of the particular culture represented by the congregation through the offering of classes in Swedish. Recently, the role of church-affiliated schools has increased and now includes several modern schools such as Queen of Peace (formerly Sacred Heart) School and St. Paul's Academy.

Many of the local churches provided basic education as well as religious instruction. This photograph shows the graduating class of 1931 at Our Lady of the Sacred Heart School.

Photo by Olaf Olson

The 1950 St. Andrew's Episcopal Church confirmation class consisted of (left to right) Lynn Walter, Lynette Evans, Gretchen Kalbrener, Elizabeth Boquist, Gail Golden, Rev. Sage, Frank Anderson, Tom Kalbrener, and Terry Golden.

Public education developed slowly in early Cloquet as depicted in this photograph of the first graduating class of Cloquet High School in 1897. The commencement exercise for the two students (Helen A. Johnson and Agnes M. Forslund) was held at the local opera house and an admission of fifteen cents was charged for all those who attended.

Modern educational facilities are more efficient than the mission schools or the first two-room public school built in Cloquet in 1883. Present-day public schools include two modern elementary schools, a middle school and a high school. Also, the former Garfield Elementary School has been extensively renovated and now functions as a community center and special education facility. The number of elementary schools has declined from five to two, perhaps reflecting the downturn in school age population following the so-called "baby boom" after World War II.

A group of early Cloquet teachers about 1898. Notice the youthful appearance of many of those pictured here. Most early school teachers only had a year or two of academic preparation before beginning their teaching careers. Most were unmarried women. In fact, it was widely held that one could not be married and be a good teacher. That unique notion persisted well into the twentieth century.

This photograph of the teaching staff at Churchill Elementary School, taken in 1963-64, shows a predominantly female staff. The idea that only women could be effective elementary school teachers was still prevalent at the time.

Back Row, left to right: Rose Kaner, Velma Odegaard, Joan Martinson, Ruth Rosted, Don Bourdeau, Ellen Nelson, Esther Brekke, Evelyn Lundblad
Front Row, left to right: Shirley Bushey, Sylvia Rud, Margaret Ann Peterson, Aili Siltanen, Elsie Erickson, Ardis Botner, Karen Lund

The Jefferson Elementary School on Cloquet Avenue between Eighth and Ninth streets, was a substantial building constructed with the best available materials. The building, completed in 1923, was intended to serve the elementary student population living in the central part of Cloquet.

An early class picture taken in the fall or winter on the steps outside of the pre-fire Washington School. The students are posing in their best clothes for this important occasion.

Note the contrast between Don Kronemann's 1962 Washington Elementary School sixth grade class and the early class picture above. The casual appearance of the students in this photograph belies the importance of the occasion.

The L.F. Leach Elementary School, completed in 1919, was intended to serve students living in the western part of Cloquet. All schools that were built in the community at that time were situated within reasonable walking distance of their intended occupants. Although bus service was available, no mass transit facilities were provided for students living within the city limits. Only those students living outside the city limits were transported by bus.

The Cloquet School District has had four high school buildings throughout its history. The first structure, pictured here, was a typical school design popular at the end of the nineteenth century. Common characteristics for school buildings at that time included large windows for natural light in the classrooms and a hip roof.

Cloquet's second high school building was dedicated on April 22, 1918, just before the disastrous fire which swept through the town. A third building, of similar design, was built on the site located at Sixth Street and Carlton Avenue. Following the Second World War, a large addition was constructed on the west side of the high school. The high school was centrally located for the convenience of students from every part of town. This building now houses the Cloquet Middle School.

Cloquet's fourth high school building was constructed on two levels and located in the southeast part of the city in a spacious wooded setting. Designed to showcase natural building materials, controversy occurred from the beginning over the construction materials, the location of the building, and the safety of the students and staff. Public concern was heightened when the building accidentally caught fire even before it was completed. A new addition, including a spacious gymnasium, was opened in 2003.

Cloquet's Public Library provides an important adjunct to the educational mission of the public and private schools. The picture, taken in the 1920s, shows a librarian giving a presentation to a group of school age students.

From the beginning, the community has emphasized learning. Many local industries encouraged students by providing summer employment to area graduates who pursued advanced training in a technical field or who sought a college education. In recent years, Cloquet has enjoyed an additional boost from the Fond du Lac Tribal and Community College. Here students can pursue a two-year associate degree. Also new four-year degree programs will soon be offered in some disciplines.

The emphasis on learning also included provision for a public library. The first library was built in 1895. In 1902 the old library was replaced by a new brownstone structure that was later destroyed in the fire that swept through Cloquet in 1918. After the fire, the Shaw Memorial Library was built on the site of the old library. Named for one of Cloquet's first sawmill operators, the library served the community for many years. Ultimately the collections outgrew the capacity of the Shaw Memorial Library, and a new facility was built in 1987 adjacent to the Garfield School on Fourteenth Street. The new library has room for a much larger collection of books, a modern reference section, computers, and meeting rooms.

Reading and other self-improvement activities were also encouraged outside of a formal academic or library setting. For example the Women's Friday Club was founded in 1914, as a study and discussion group. In more recent years an active community education program has evolved that offers

The Cloquet Public Library moved into its new building on 14th Street in 1987.

Photo by Marlene Wisuri, 1995

local residents many varied opportunities to improve skills or explore new fields.

Religious and educational organizations were not the only institutions that flourished in Cloquet. Various social organizations such as theatrical groups, bands and choruses (both civic and ethnic), clubs, and fraternal organizations attracted members. Interest in culture and local history also led to the foundation of the Carlton County Historical Society in 1949.

Entertainment has always been important in Cloquet. Several theaters have existed in the community over the years. The Bijou, the Diamond Theater, the Grand, and the Nelson Opera House were all important community attractions. In addition to live theater and vaudeville, one could also be entertained by the new motion picture shows.

The Bijou, later renamed the LEB Theater, with its orchestra pit and stage, hosted both "live" performances complete with musical accompaniment and motion pictures. At first the motion pictures were relatively short productions and were used to fill space between regular live acts. Until the introduction of sound motion pictures in the late 1920s, the theater pianist provided appropriate accompaniment to many silent movies. The LEB Theater and the Cloquet Theater (later renamed the Chief Theater) catered to moviegoers with regular feature films. The ten cent Saturday matinee was also a popular diversion for both young and old in the era before television.

Organizations like the Saturday Musicale offered residents an opportunity to hear musical presentations in a refined setting. In this photograph, taken in the 1950s, the membership is gathered for a reception following the conclusion of the featured program.

Other organizations for which the community has long been noted include musical groups. Parades, for which the town is famous, and band concerts provided entertainment to many residents over the years. It is interesting to note that shortly before World War I the community boasted a first-class city band and the local Finnish population also fielded an imposing brass band. In more recent times a drum and bugle corps, a scout band, and the Cloquet High School Band, as well as fine vocal groups like the Viking Male Chorus, added to the musical array.

The Cloquet Chapter of the Royal Neighbors, shown here in Scottish dress, was photographed in the 1920s. Notice the rolled down hose worn by the ladies, in keeping with the flapper image of the time.

From the earliest years of the city civic organizations filled the need for social outlets. The local Masonic Lodge and the Order of the Eastern Star were organized in the 1890s. The Women's Catholic Order of Foresters was founded in 1898 and a YMCA was organized in 1900. Other groups such as the Loyal Order of the Moose and the Rotary Club are of more recent origin.

Other groups, such as veterans organizations formed after the two World Wars, also contributed to the civic life of the community. They joined older organizations, many of which had strong ethnic ties, such as the Sons and Daughters of Norway, formed in 1906.

The various social groups not only held regular meetings and local events, but also sponsored picnics and camping excursions into the surrounding countryside. They often traveled equipped with tents and folding army cots. The participants in these events traveled by car caravan in case of breakdown. Through billowing clouds of dust and over rugged gravel roads they journeyed to nearby Chub Lake and Big Lake. The more daring ventured further afield to such places as Eagle Lake south of Cromwell, or Round Lake and Sandy Lake in Aitkin County.

The Ladies of Kaleva pose for a group picture in the 1960s. Styles have changed but group pictures of organization members retain a certain familiar quality.

Photo by Siebold Photography

These early excursions, unlike today's weekend trips, took longer and were not accomplished without difficulty. One notorious rite of passage for those traveling by automobile over Trunk Highway 2 (also known as the Moorhead Road) to the western reaches of Carlton County occurred immediately north of Wild Rice Lake. There, on what is now an abandoned roadway, the lead car always stopped and the driver or some other brave soul took off shoes and socks and waded through puddles to determine if the water was low enough so as not to short out the ignition coils. This event was only one of the many joys incidental to such excursions.

Of course not all time was spent in pleasure. Certain organizations took a great interest in social issues. Among these groups were the labor unions that were organized to achieve improved working conditions. The labor movement has always been a strong and vital part of the community. The Cloquet Labor Temple at Fourteenth Street and Avenue C has for many years been a symbol of the community's interest in labor and social issues.

Political issues were also important to the community. Early issues, such as women's suffrage or temperance, may seem archaic today; however at the beginning of the twentieth century they were matters of great concern to which most people could relate. Over the years many political parties have taken their cues from local organizations that were formed to deal with specific matters of concern to the community.

One type of organization grew in response to both political and social issues—the cooperative movement. The simple idea of pooling one's resources for the betterment of the entire membership rapidly caught on. The Cloquet Cooperative Society quickly became the largest organization of its kind. The local co-op not only supplied the material needs of its membership with groceries, hardware, and other necessary items, but also sponsored various forms of cultural entertainment. Plays, poetry readings, speakers, concerts, and dances were all regular features of the Cloquet Cooperative Society.

The institutions and organizations that grew up in Cloquet over the decades have for the most part proven to be quite durable. They are the glue that binds us everyone.

Organizations such as the Finnish Temperance Society helped instill the virtue of abstinence. The Temperance Hall, shown in this 1916 photograph, was situated on lower Ninth Street.

Photo courtesy of Vilma Siltanen Autio

The local YMCA offered the residents of Cloquet a place to meet, play games, and participate in sports. The first building, pictured here at the turn of the twentieth century, was built entirely of wood and was consumed by fire in 1918.

The interior of Cloquet's first YMCA was well-lighted and featured elaborately carved and heavily varnished woodwork. Note the billiard table in the background.

Photo by Octavie Morneau

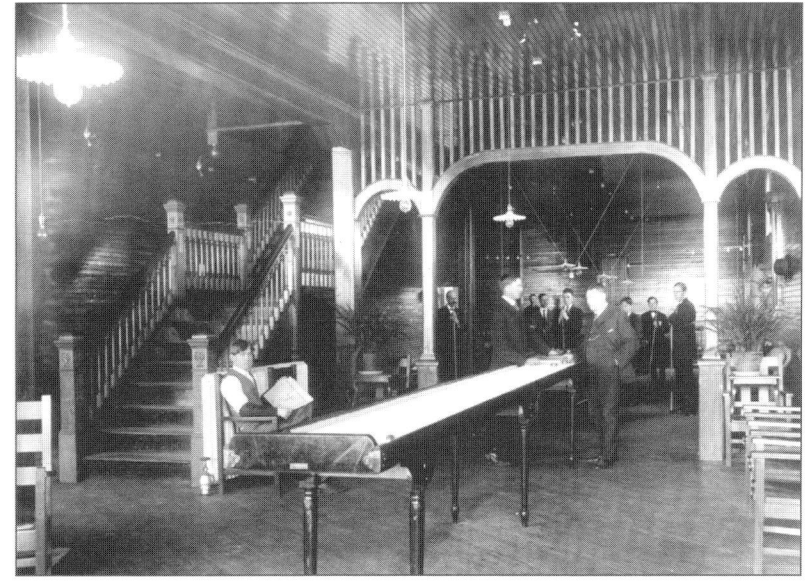

This photograph shows the Cloquet Gymnastic Team in action. It was most likely taken at the High School prior to the Fire of 1918.

The Cloquet City Band, shown here in this early twentieth century photograph, has apparently gathered at the railroad depot to either serenade the passengers or welcome some visiting dignitary.

Photo by Octavie Morneau

In addition to having a first-class City Band and a High School Band, Cloquet also had a Finnish brass band. Only a few members are identified in this photograph dating from about 1913. Seated on the extreme left is Alfred Lumppio. Axel Hoffren is fifth from the left. In the back row Bill Syralia (also known as Syrjälä) and Arvid Rahiikinen are fourth and fifth from the left and Eric Lindquist is seventh from the left. On the extreme right is Emil Luukkonen. Most of the members of this band also belonged to the City Band.

Musical organizations were popular in early Cloquet, The LEB Theater Orchestra posed for the camera in this photo taken in the 1920s. The members are, left to right, Nelly Everson Johnson, Bill Syralia, Matt Killpu (sp.?), and "Snowball" Johnson.

The LEB Theater was one of several theaters in Cloquet. According to the theater marquee it was also "The Home Of The Big Pipe Organ." In addition to regular vaudeville acts and feature films, the Cloquet High School Operetta was routinely performed on its stage.

Dance bands such as "Nick's Cavaliers," shown in this 1930 photograph, were extremely popular and played for a wide variety of events in Cloquet and the surrounding area. Instruments, such as the banjo and sousaphone, were favored because they could project sound easily. The mutes used on the brass instruments gave the music of the time a distinctive sound. In an era before portable amplification systems were commonplace, some vocalists used megaphones to project their voices in large dance halls.

Photo by McComb Studio

Interest in music apparently came at an early age as depicted in this picture of the Leach Kindergarten Rhythm Band taken in 1934. Note the elaborate costume of the band leader complete with hussar breeches and jacket.

Photo by Olaf Olson

The Viking Male Chorus, shown in this 1958 photograph, needed no amplification equipment to make their voices heard. The group sang for many years and was quite popular in the community.

Civic groups frequently took advantage of educational programs or outings. Pictured here is the Cloquet Rotary Club picnic at the University of Minnesota Cloquet Forest Experimental Station in the 1920s.
Photo by Olaf Olson

The Cloquet Rotary Club remains an important civic organization. This 1998 photo pictures members of the group at Fauley Park. The Rotary has "adopted" care of the park as a service project.

Sometimes tours or social outings took the participants a great distance, as was the case with this Cloquet Commercial Club visit to Tamarack, Minnesota, by car caravan in the early 1920s. Note the club banners on the cars parked along main street. Even though the route of travel lay over a trunk highway, there were few repair facilities along the way. Wise motorists traveled in caravans to avoid being stranded if one's car broke down.

Photo courtesy of Marjorie Roeschlein

Most outings were relatively close to town as in this scene at Camp Coy on Big Lake in the 1920s. Note the bathing costumes and caps.

Organizations often become involved with fund-raising to support their activities. In this 1983 photo the Jaycee Women (later Women of Today) raise money and have fun at a car wash on Cloquet Avenue.

Labor organizations also had facilities for social gatherings. Shown here is the Finnish Workers' Hall on Eleventh Street and Avenue F before the Fire of 1918.

An architect's sketch of the proposed Labor Temple located on north Fourteenth Street.

Plans were drafted for a new union hall in the 1950s. The new building was to be known as the "Labor Temple," and this photograph depicts the dedication ceremony for the building complete with live radio broadcast on WKLK Radio.

73

Some businesses and organizations were sponsored by local industries. This 1908 photograph shows the interior of the "Cloquet Lumber Company's Big Store." In the foreground are coal stoves and woodburning kitchen ranges with warming pans and hot water reservoirs. The "Big Store" tried to woo customers by having a large inventory and variety of merchandise.

The Cloquet Independent.

Vol. 3.   CLOQUET, MINN., 20 JUNE, 1901.   NO. 52.

CLOQUET LUMBER CO.'S BIG STORE.

Are We In It? Well, We Guess. Appreciating the truth that "we are in it," the first question in return would naturally be, "Are you in it?" If not, do you propose to get "next" to a good thing? We have it — it is your fault if you don't have it. Our announcement of Genuine Cut Price Bargains to be found below should attract your undivided attention and receive your earnest and careful consideration.

DRY GOODS DEPT.

Shirt Waists.
All our shirt waists in white, black and colors will be sold at actual cost. They are handsome and in the latest styles.

Silks.
We have a fine line of silks, silk flannels, taffeta and wash silks which we are offering at a special discount of 10 per cent while they last.

Ginghams.
Our large assortment of ginghams is very fine. Zephyr ginghams in check and stripe, regular 10c quality, are going at 7c.

Batists.
Embroidered in pink, blue, and red. 12½c quality at 10c. Nothing like them ever shown in Cloquet for the price.

Wash Goods.
Pois Mignon Brilliant, a handsome fabric in the latest shades, suitable for dresses and shirt waists, 20c quality at 16c.

Skirts.
Our entire line of ladies skirts will be closed out at cost.

Shoe Department.
Don't forget to inspect our shoe dept. We carry a full line of ladies, men's and children's shoes and we quote figures to interest you.

Carpets.
When you want your rooms carpeted, give us a call. Particular attention given to this dept. Carpets matched and sewed ready to put down.

REMEMBER!

These prices will prevail for a limited period, only. You cannot afford to let such bargains go by and we don't want you to do so. Such inducements as we here offer you should receive your unqualified approval.

GROCERY DEPT.

Flour.
Every housekeeper is familiar with Pillsbury's Best and Washburn & Crosby's Gold Medal flour. They are the leading brands. You may have either...

An advertisement for the Cloquet Lumber Company's Big Store published in the *Cloquet Independent*, June 20, 1901. The variety of products offered for sale included such diverse items as shirts, shoes, skirts, carpets, flour, and syrup in sixteen pound wooden pails. Since it was a company owned store one could buy on credit. The *Cloquet Independent* was a short-lived local newspaper that provided competition for the *Pine Knot* for a time.

...berries will be vastly benefitted in getting our prices. Michigan and Wisconsin berries arriving daily. They will not last long.

The "Big Store" was not the only big store in Cloquet. The cooperative movement was very strong in Cloquet and the surrounding county. The Cloquet Cooperative Society maintained two large stores and several specialty businesses in town. Shown here is the Co-op Store Number Two located on the corner of Broadway and Avenue C.

This picture shows the interior of Co-op Store Number Two with staff and merchandise. Many citizens patronized the stores because of their reputation for a large variety of quality products at reasonable prices.

Photo by McComb Studio

There were many advantages to living in communities like Cloquet. Perhaps one of the most delightful benefits was the variety of entertainment such as holiday parades. This early parade was probably a Fourth of July event, judging by the bunting and prominent display of flags. People came from miles around to see such spectacles. Note the six-horse team pulling the elaborate float.

Chapter Four
Village Life

One of the outstanding features that has always set life in the city of Cloquet apart from a rural existence is the amazing variety of amenities available to the people of the community. From the very beginning of the village in the 1880s to the present time, residents have enjoyed services rarely found outside of the community such as public waterworks, sewer service, paved streets and sidewalks, and fire and police protection.

Additional features like electric lighting, manufactured gas service, twice-daily mail delivery, and telephone service (provided by two competing companies) were common during the first decades of the twentieth century. Of course all of these new services came with a price. For example, the meter men who read the electric, gas, and water meters, became the focus of humor. Although the meter men saved the homeowner many needless steps, these officials quickly became the butt of off-color jokes. In fact, stories about the housewife and the meter man were a staple in every radio show, vaudeville act, and some popular songs of the day. So much for public service.

Cloquet was surrounded by small family farms that provided the community with many different products, such as vegetables, meat, milk, butter, and eggs. Grunig's farm, located near the intersection of Stanley Avenue and Fourteenth Street, was a good example of the kind of agriculture practiced in the area.

Until a few years ago, one common scene in Cloquet that certainly set city life apart from a rural existence was the family-owned corner grocery store. There was a "corner store" in every neighborhood where merchants stocked all the necessary household items as well as "vital" supplies of penny candy and other treats. In these establishments cash discounts were the norm. Some stores even offered home delivery service for telephone orders received from busy homes, something virtually unheard of today with our large discount stores.

This busy street scene in early Cloquet includes a group of people riding into town in a buggy pulled by oxen. The trip probably took awhile, but the chance to visit friends and shop at the local stores far outweighed any inconvenience. The women crossing the street in the foreground appear to be curious about the intent of the photographer.

Photo by Octavie Morneau

Of course home delivery and other services were not confined solely to the proprietors of small corner stores. Two large grocery stores operated by the Cloquet Cooperative Society provided citizens of early Cloquet with an amazing variety of commodities at reasonable prices together with home delivery.

Besides the neighborhood store, a veritable parade of vendors visited the homemaker during a typical week. Such products as ice, milk and dairy products, eggs, fresh fruits and vegetables were all delivered to the home. Specialty products, such as those offered by the Fuller Brush Company, the Jewel Tea Company, and Watkins Products were brought into the family living room where the homemaker could choose from an amazing array of samples.

Like their rural counterparts, the busy city homeowners could also resort to purchasing from mail-order companies like the venerable Sears Roebuck or the former Montgomery Ward Company. Voluminous catalogues from these and other mail-order sources were a delight to every member of the household. In the early years of the twentieth century, the family larder was both a common and essential part of the home and pantries were periodically restocked with essential items which were usually bought in bulk from either a mail-order house or a local store.

Until the middle of the twentieth century the entire emphasis of the merchant, whether he sold from a local store, mail-order house, or door to door, was bringing goods and services to the home, rather than requiring the homeowner's coming to the merchant. Merchandising, at least as far as it applies to many common items used at home, has changed remarkably in the last several decades. Gone is the corner store. It has largely been replaced in Cloquet

A typical corner store in a Cloquet neighborhood around the time of the First World War. Note the flags prominently displayed in the store window and on the home across the street.

Home grocery delivery from Kolseth & Anderson was by horse and wagon in the summer and by sleigh in winter. Driver Carl Lind, and an unidentified passenger, pose for the camera with one of the horses used by Kolseth's. The store purchased the Cloquet Fire Department's horses shortly after the Fire of 1918. After a busy day, the animals would be unhitched and allowed to run on the streets. Local residents long remembered how those spirited horses would race by. In winter, boys would try to catch a ride on the delivery sleigh, but Lind would touch his horse with the reins just as the nearest lad reached for the rear of the sleigh. He left many in the dust.

by large retail outlets, a modern mall, and specialty stores. Some door-to-door sales continue to this day, but this method accounts for only a part of current sales. Such are the changes confronting us today.

Some stores, such as the Cloquet Co-op Store Number One, used delivery trucks like those shown here parked on Avenue F. Two of the vehicles are McCormack-Deering delivery trucks and the one on the right appears to be an International. The date on the license plate of the left vehicle looks like 1923.

Another interesting aspect of village life can be seen in the number and types of living accommodations. While the vast majority of residents now live in comfortable homes, a significant percentage of Cloquet's population during its early years lived in boarding houses or hotels. Many of the names of the facilities have survived, although the structures have not. Places such as the Cloquet Boarding House, the Oswald House, the O'Donnell House, the Northern Lumber Company Boarding House, the McKinnon House, and the Toivola Company especially catered to the large bachelor population in the community. Most of the residents were either lumberjacks or sawmill workers.

Residents and staff of the Toivola Company boarding house on Avenue F pose for a group picture. Boarding houses such as the Toivola, catered to mill workers and lumberjacks. This building is still in use as an apartment building.

While one might be tempted to see the large number of boarding houses as indicative of a highly transient population, it was quite characteristic of many early sawmill towns to have a large number of facilities for the bachelor population. The boarding houses not only offered accommodations but also provided three generous home-cooked meals a day with plenty of extra treats and an endless supply of hot coffee for snacks between meals.

Although boarding facilities were offered to the ordinary lumberjack or mill hand, more lavish accommodations were provided for visiting company officials and sales personnel. In many respects, some of the "company houses" maintained by the mills in Cloquet had all the amenities of the familiar boarding house.

In the early years, Cloquet boasted several regular hotels such as the Freeman Hotel, Montreal Hotel, and the Northeastern Hotel. Ordinary travelers needed a place to stay and most of them found accommodations in one of the early hotels. Some boarding houses also took in salesmen or travelers, but most opted for a steady clientele—especially one composed of the well-paid bachelor lumberjack and mill worker.

Of course those well-paid bachelor lumberjacks and mill hands also sought other types of entertainment and refreshment outside of the boarding house setting. Cloquet was famous, nay notorious, for its establishments meant to cater to the lumberjacks. Plenty of stories abound of the various saloons located on Dunlap Island. The Northeastern Hotel and the Moose Saloon were two of many noted landmarks on "the island."

The Solem Hotel, built after the fire, provided rooms for visiting business men and travelers. Also many of the single teachers in the Cloquet schools lived at the hotel.

It should be remembered that of all the establishments located on Dunlap Island, perhaps none other has served in so many different roles as the Northeastern Hotel. Its stated function was that of a hotel, but the establishment also included a saloon and dining facilities. During the period immediately following the disastrous fire that swept through Cloquet in the fall of 1918, the Northeastern Hotel also served as a makeshift hospital where burn victims, as well as others in need of medical attention, could seek relief. In more recent years, the building served as a movie backdrop. Today, the Northeastern survives as an enduring reminder of the early years of Cloquet.

The role of the Northeastern Hotel as a makeshift medical facility serves to highlight another amenity enjoyed by the citizens of Cloquet. Over the years, the residents of the community have benefited from a number of available medical facilities. These have ranged from small, family-oriented facilities to the current Community Memorial Hospital, which is presently undergoing a major expansion.

Some of the early medical facilities that operated in Cloquet were located in private homes modified to serve as hospitals. Such facilities were intended to serve a special type of clientele such as expectant mothers; other hospitals were more general in nature. All of the early hospitals, however, fulfilled a necessary function throughout their existence.

There were other characteristics of Cloquet's civic life that were notable, including its city parks.

The Northeastern Hotel, as it appeared in 1976. The building has served many purposes throughout its history in addition to the primary use as a saloon, hotel and restaurant.

Throughout its history, Cloquet has hosted many communal events. Such celebrations ranged from Fourth of July parades and fireworks displays to picnics and band concerts. Many of these events were centered in Pinehurst Park. In fact, "the park," as some residents referred to it, was the focal point of the community in the early years. Pinehurst Park is still an attraction today as a setting for concerts, festivals, and sports events.

Parades invariably originated in Pinehurst Park. Civic celebrations of holidays such as Memorial Day, the Fourth of July, and Labor Day all featured extensive parades. In time, Cloquet's parades, with their many colorful floats, marching bands, and drill teams, became famous throughout the region and attracted people from surrounding communities to the city.

All of Cloquet's city parks were showpieces of civic pride. They were well decorated with flower beds and attractive ornamental plantings interspersed with local specimen trees. In fact, the frequent use of native conifers to set off the park landscape was typical of the town's parks. Flower-lined drives, such as the one around Pinehurst Park's two ponds, complemented the beauty of the surrounding landscape. Even the city hall boasted a colorful floral display and the initials of the Cloquet Fire Department, "CFD," were spelled out in front of the old fire department building in multicolored pansies for all to see.

Cloquet's city parks flourished under the care of Parks Superintendent Tony LaTulip in the 1940s and 50s. The centerpiece of this floral display is actually an illuminated horse trough moved to Pinehurst Park from Second Street.

Some of the parks featured such refinements as tennis courts and ball fields. Several parks also sported ornamental horse troughs for the many horses used for transportation by both local residents and businesses. In later years some of these troughs were used as gigantic planting boxes for the many colorful floral displays so long a trademark of Cloquet's parks and public buildings.

Cloquet residents have always been great sports fans, and so much park space was devoted to various athletic activities. Skiing, birling, baseball, and more recently, hockey, have been extremely popular. Several ski slides, baseball diamonds, and a modern hockey shelter have been erected over the years. Birling, or log rolling, was performed on the pond in Pinehurst Park or on local lakes.

Whatever the changing tastes in sporting events, Cloquet has always participated in and frequently fielded winning teams for various events. Over the years more land has been set aside for keeping open space and parks available for all the residents of the community.

New park space on Dunlap Island, scene of much early civic activity, has been developed. Veterans' Park and hiking paths along the north side of the St. Louis River attest to the desire to retain some open areas as well as natural settings for the benefit of both visitors and the local population. Ironically, the community, which was once so focused on the businesses along the riverfront for its livelihood, has now once again embraced the scenic vistas of the St. Louis River as the focus for some of its newest parks.

These then are a few of the amenities of city life as it was and still is in Cloquet. In spite of the passing decades, there remains a certain continuity within all of the various aspects of city life described here. While certain day-to-day routines have changed, the basic pattern of village life remains remarkably constant.

> In spite of the passing decades, there remains a certain continuity within all of the various aspects of city life. While certain day-to-day routines have changed, the basic pattern of village life remains remarkably constant.

One advantage of living in Cloquet was the public waterworks system. The prospect of laboring at a hand pump or carrying buckets of water was eliminated with the completion of the central water system. This early picture shows the beginning of construction on the tower legs.

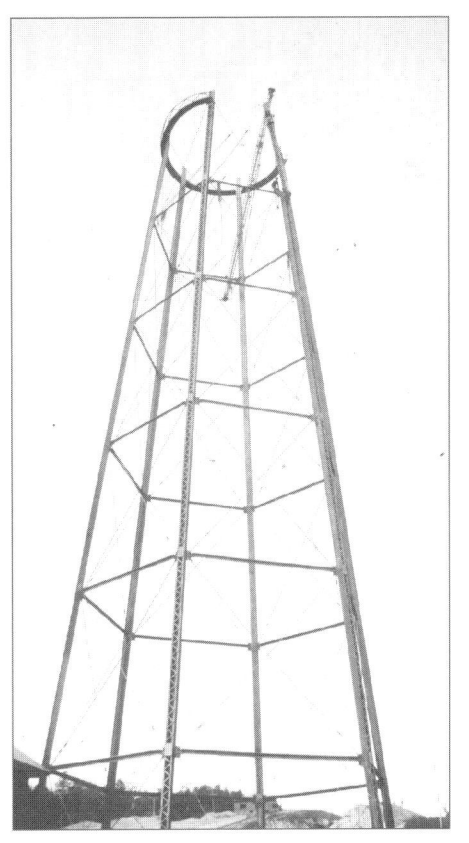

The tower is almost completed.

The erection of Cloquet's distinctive water tower in 1908, was recorded on film in various phases of construction.

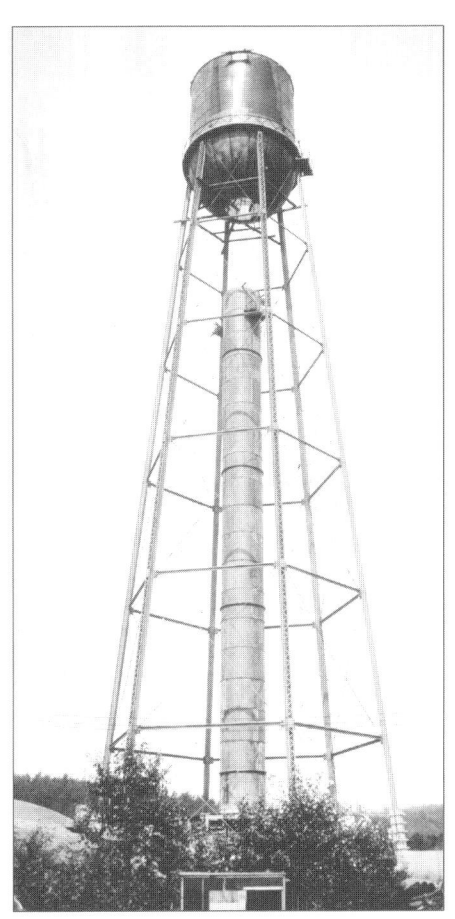

This last photograph shows the central portion of the water tower. Only one or two more sections of pipe and the cover of the tank remain to be fastened in place.

Cloquet has always derived its water supply from deep wells. In the 1960s, however, it was believed that Lake Superior could provide a more dependable supply of water. The picture here shows the groundbreaking ceremony for the construction of the Cloquet Water Line. The completed project did not fully live up to its promise because of the water quality.

Fire protection, along with a dependable water supply, was another advantage of city life. The history of the Cloquet Fire Department goes back to the summer of 1887, when the village accepted a bid from the Boston Woven Hose Company for one thousand feet of hose, four hose carts, four thirty-inch pipes (nozzles), and twelve spanner wrenches, for the sum of $835. By the beginning of the twentieth century, the fire department boasted three horse-drawn fire wagons and a fire hall as shown in this picture.

Fire department personnel, shown here in the summer of 1937, pose with their open cab pumper outside the new fire hall on the corner of Seventh Street and Cloquet Avenue.
The firemen pictured from left to right are William Hauptmann, Lawrence Bergeron, Kenneth Walker, and Ray Poirer. Chief Lester Clark is standing next to the Chief's car with an unidentified person.

By 1962, the fire department had grown to fourteen full-time fire fighters. The crew, pictured here with Cloquet Fire Chief Arnold M. Luukkonen, pose with one of their powerful new pumpers. Luukkonen brought the fire department to a high point of efficiency with state-of-the-art equipment while remaining within budget. In addition, he organized the volunteer fire departments in the surrounding townships and villages into an effective force that could swell the ranks of local firefighters in any emergency.

Other men in uniform could also be found on the streets of Cloquet. Shown here are Cloquet's postmen posing in front of their delivery truck. The men made their rounds on foot and residents enjoyed twice-daily mail delivery.
Pictured are, left to right standing, Clarence Scheibe, William Boyer, Edwin C. Nelson, Joseph Pastika, and Harry Nordquist. Kneeling is Harry Kaner, who became the mayor of Cloquet in 1932.

Cloquet's first policeman and first police chief was John McSweeney. McSweeney started out as village Street Commissioner, a position he held for seven years before becoming "night policeman." It was said of McSweeney that "He is jolly and good natured as the world goes, as ready to chaff you as to put you in the calaboose. But when he nails you the 'jig is up'. " Officer McSweeney, pictured here with uniform and badge, was an imposing figure. He patrolled the streets of Cloquet on foot or on bicycle.

Cloquet's streets were bordered with concrete sidewalks, curbs and gutters, but the streets themselves were not paved. To combat the dust created by passing vehicles, the city resorted to a water sprinkler wagon. Alex Anakkala, shown here with his team of horses, hired out to the city to drive the Cloquet Street Department's sprinkler wagon. By the 1920s, the city began paving the streets by spraying hot tar over the gravel. Although the tar surface solved the problem of dust, it stuck to the shoes of pedestrians on hot summer days.

87

Snow removal on residential streets became mechanized in the late 1920s. Today modern motor graders, like the one shown here, or heavy trucks with plows, keep the streets snow free.
Photo by Timothy J. Krohn

Winter posed a unique set of problems for the Street Department. Snow removal was accomplished either by special plows or by gangs of residents with shovels. The winter of 1922 was accompanied by heavy snow, as shown in this photograph looking west along Cloquet Avenue. The new Shaw Memorial Library is to the left and the Cloquet Lumber Company's horse barns and drying yards are to the right.

Cloquet boasted a Western Union Telegraph Office. Shown here is Henry H. Gellerman, seated at the telegraph. Note the sounding device to his right and the typewriter used to type out the messages received over the wire. In the background, a delivery boy takes a phone call while Mr. Gellerman studies the text of a message.

Cloquet, like so many other busy cities, had a central telephone exchange. In fact, for a time the city boasted two competing telephone companies. This picture, taken some time in the 1950s, shows a typical row of operators working manual switchboards. One could call "Central" for the time any time of day. The simple act of lifting the receiver from the hook always brought a cheery "Number please!"

Fourth of July parades were always a big event in Cloquet. The marching band shown in this 1928 photograph appears to be outfitted in white canvas sailor caps.

My how times change. This Fourth of July parade forty years later featured a group of Shriners from AAD Temple driving their fleet of snowmobiles down Chestnut Street. The machines were specially equipped with wheels for use on hard-paved surfaces

Photo by Harold Olson

A winter ice skating scene on the frozen lake in Pinehurst Park, the oldest of the city parks. Note the warming house on the left of the picture below the wooden pavilion and the almost complete absence of trees or other landscape features.

Ice skating on the frozen park lake continued to be a favorite pastime. Pinehurst Park at one time featured two lakes with a winding drive bordered with trees and manicured flower beds. Today, only one of the original lakes survives.

Photo by Harold Olson

City parks were not the only venue for celebrations or special events. This scene, taken at the intersection of Seventh Street and Cloquet Avenue in the 1920s, shows a dog team preparing to race down Cloquet Avenue. The buildings shown behind the dog team are the Cloquet Lumber Company's horse barns.

Every city, at one time or another, has had band concerts in the park and Cloquet was no exception. Band concerts in Pinehurst Park like this performance by the Cloquet High School Band were well attended.

Photo by Harold Olson

Cloquet residents and visitors enjoyed carnivals in Pinehurst Park. Fourth of July and Labor Day usually included celebrations in the park such as shown in this photograph.

Photo by Harold Olson

Birling, or log rolling, was very popular in Cloquet with both men and women. Shown here is the 1917 Cloquet women's team complete with distinctive team uniforms. Four of the five ladies have been identified. They are from left to right, Hannah Hagen, unknown, Marion Jesse Johnson, Frances O'Meara Childs, and Helen LaVoi.

The Cloquet Women's Golf Club is shown in this 1933 photograph. Seated from left to right are Winifred Campbell, Kathleen Kenety, Maxine Dolan, Marion Ward, Elsie Kaner, Camilla Campbell, and Ruth McNair. Standing from left to right are Leone Kelly, Madge Sandstrom, Kathryn Davis, Ruth Olin, Virginia Spafford, Margaret Driscoll, Gunelle Husby, Edith Norman, and Ava Kenety.

Photo by Olaf Olson

Various businesses and organizations sponsored sports teams such as the Cloquet Co-op Bowling Team shown in this 1940 photograph.

Photo by Olaf Olson

Cloquet produced several outstanding birlers. Joe Conner, shown here "cuffing the bubbles" in 1940, was one well-known champion.

Cloquet's first football team, shown here on October 9th, 1904, was sponsored by the Cloquet Athletic Club.

"Indoor Baseball," or what we today call softball, was popular at the beginning of the twentieth century. Cloquet's championship team, sponsored by the Northwest Paper Company, is pictured here in 1920.

The Cloquet High School women's basketball team of 1912 pose for a picture with their coach. Note the colorful uniforms complete with bloomers.

Baseball has always been America's pastime. Shown here is the 1911 Cloquet Baseball Team. Members included, from left to right, Ned Blinn, Toge Rogentine, Albert Bonneville, Doctor Carl Sandstrom, Henfen Carlson, Julius Carlson, Evelyn McKenna, Simore Loisel, Paul Leonard, Emil Buskala, and Al Gaskill.

Pictured here around 1910 is the Finnish Athletic Association of Cloquet. Lying in the front is Einar Reponen. Einar, along with many other Cloquet boys, enlisted to fight in World War I. Unfortunately, a double tragedy occurred in Einar's case. He died during the war and his remains were shipped home in a casket. The casket arrived at the Cloquet railroad depot on October 11th, 1918. Most of the town, including the depot and Einar's coffin, was completely consumed by fire the next day, Saturday, October 12th, 1918.

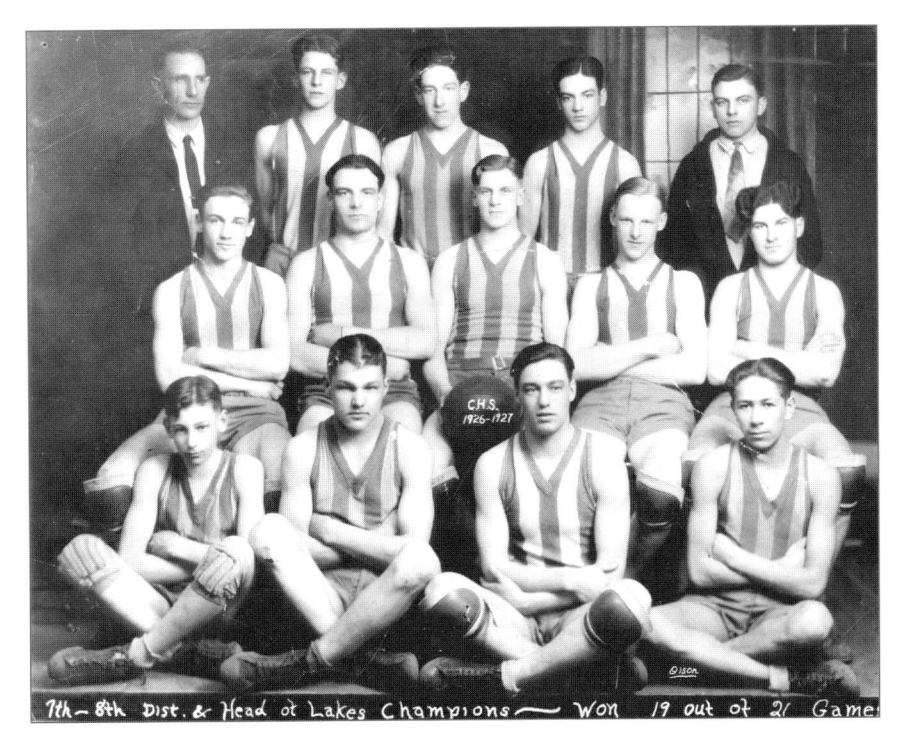

The Cloquet High School basketball team of 1926-27. Coach Herb Drew, shown on the left in the back row, was a longtime figure in school sports.

Photo by Olaf Olson

Herb Drew probably photographing one of his teams.

Thirty years later, Coach Drew, now High School Athletic Director, posed with the 1957 Cloquet High School Football Team. He is standing second from the left in row two.

Cloquet has produced some noted athletes in the last century such as boxer Herbert J. Hubert and Olympic skier Mike Randall shown ready to jump in a winter ski competition at Lake Placid in 1984.

This happy group of Cloquet trap shooters has just brought home a handsome trophy.
Pictured in back, left to right, are Morrie Berg, Bob Minogue, Charles Golen, Wayne Crider.
In front are Dave Golen, Harry Berg.

Photo courtesy of Robert Minogue

Hockey has a long history in Cloquet. Pictured here is the first high school hockey team in 1940. Notice, with the exception of the goalies, the complete absence of any form of protective body armor or padding. Assorted fractures and missing teeth were the badges of honor for the early hockey player.

"We've come a long way baby!" Shown here is one of the first Cloquet High School women's hockey teams around 1982.

War fund drives, such as the one described on this World War I poster for May 20th to 27th, 1918, appealed to the folks at home to support the troops. The goal set forth in this poster was to raise $20,000.

Chapter Five
War, Disaster, and Depression

Cloquet's history is not without its sober side. The community, like many others throughout the nation, experienced calamities both natural and man-made. Cloquet was barely into its second decade as a city when a series of events occurred which had a major impact on the future of the community.

In August of 1914, political events in Europe precipitated the outbreak of the First World War. While the United States was not directly involved in the war until 1917, still the impact of the worldwide conflict was felt in many different ways. Demand for war materiel, such as the forest products produced in Cloquet, to equip the various belligerent powers increased markedly.

With America's entry into the conflict on April 6th, 1917, ever larger amounts of resources were called for. The commencement of open hostilities with certain of the belligerent powers also meant that men from Cloquet and the surrounding area were needed to swell the ranks of the United States military forces. No longer was the central issue merely one of supplying goods; now human life was at risk.

In Cloquet, as elsewhere, most thoughts were focused on winning "the war to end all wars." News bulletins from the western front in Europe were eagerly scanned for information about the progress of the war and for word about local men in the armed services. In addition, newspaper accounts and photographs from the

Many young men from Cloquet served in World War I. Arthur L. Johnson, pictured here wearing his army uniform and campaign ribbon, was one of several hundred who fought in the war.

period show that residents participated in a variety of patriotic pursuits such as war bond rallies, "loyalty day" programs, parades, and the cultivation of "victory gardens."

In July and August of 1918, the tide of the war began to shift in favor of the United States and her allies. Large numbers of American troops had reached the western front and were employed in driving back enemy forces. In the process of carrying out the offensive, the men of the American Expeditionary Force sustained numerous casualties. Included in the number of dead and wounded was the first man from Cloquet killed in action, Corporal Carl Anderson. Others from the community had been injured or killed by disease or in mishaps at military installations in the United States, but Anderson's death on August 12th at the Vesle River brought home to many the terrible cost of the war.

FIRST CLOQUET BOY IS KILLED IN WAR

Carl L. Anderson, Who Enlisted in August, 1917, Falls in Action.

Newspaper notices, such as the one announcing the death of Carl L. Anderson in August of 1917, brought home the tragedy of war to local families and friends.

By the fall of 1918, the war in Europe had reached a crescendo and many rightly suspected that the conflict would soon be over. Unfortunately, a number of the political and social issues that had caused the outbreak of hostilities in the first place still remained unresolved at the conclusion of the First World War. Instead, these issues continued to simmer beneath the surface, giving rise to new animosities that eventually boiled over two decades later in the form of the Second World War.

On the home front, there were also numerous social and political issues that remained unresolved. For example, prior to the outbreak of hostilities, the question of women's suffrage had been discussed by many, including the residents of Cloquet. Given the numerous contributions of women to the war effort, it now seemed only fair to extend to them the privilege of voting.

Another major social problem facing the nation and the residents of Cloquet concerned the rise of alcoholism and the growing agitation of the temperance movement and other political groups for the enactment of

LIST OF CLOQUET BOYS SERVING IN THE UNITED STATES ARMY AND NAVY.

Anderson, Henry, 20th Eng. A. E. F.
Anderson, Axel, Co. A. 46th Inft.
Anderson, Chas. L., Med. Dept. 352 Inft.
Anderson, Hialmer, Ambulance Co. 17.
Anderson, Earl E.
Anderson, Carl L., Co. I. 59th Inft.
Anderson, Geo.
Anderson, Arthur.
Anderson, Harold, Co. E. 318 Eng.
Atkinson, Roy, Co. B. 109 Eng.
Athansoff, Lazar, Co. I. 36th Inft.
Ames, Arthur, Coast Art.
Amell, John E., Honorable Discharge.
Anderson, Arthur C.
Bergquist, Harold.
Batters, Arthur J., Galley 101, 1st Reg. U. S. N. T. S.
Becklund, John, Co. E. 8th U. S. Inft.
Briant, Ammie, Batt. A. 17th F. A. A. E. F.
Barker, Griswold G., Aviation Mobilization.
Butts, Ray, 126 Areo Squad A. E. F.
Bodway, Raymond J., 12 Co. C. A. C.
Bratt, Rungnar, Med. Dept. 350 Inft.
Bengtson, Walter, Co. B. 125th Machine Gun Bat.
Boyer, Maurice, 151 U. S. F. A. Co. 76, A. E. F.
Breslin, Sylvester S., 162 Depot Brig. 1st Prov. Reg. 4
Bollin, Ed., 13th Cavalry.
Bird, Lloyd.
Blair, William, "Spruce Div."
Bru, Erne, Coast Artillery.
Boyer, Clifford, "Spruce Div."
Brunner, Leo John.
Bruno, Olaf, "Spruce Div."
Bodway, Gerald, Honorable Discharge.
Boquist, Sigurd E., died in the service.
Beck, Henry, Medical Corps, Base Hospital 39, A. E. F.
Beaulieu, Leo.
Blair, John, "Spruce Div."
Blomberg, Ray B., Aviation Signal Corps.
Bjorklund, Thuri.
Beaster, Edward.
Bonneville, Napoleon.
Bonneville, Isadore.
Beauchamp, Charles.
Couillard, Al E.
Campbell, Lieut. H. J., Co. M. 349 Inft.
Campbell, Lieut. Robert, Qt. Masters Dept., A. E. F.
Campbell, Sargt. Ross, 313 Eng. Co. D.
Case, Robert, 427 Squadron, A. S. S. C.
Chapados, Sam, Spruce Div.
Cook, Mark, 20th Eng. Spruce Div.
Cook, Percy, 20th Eng. Spruce Div.
Carey, L. W.
Coad, Matt, 125th U. S. Fld. Art. Bat. C.
Chillen, Henry.
Carson, Jack, Supply Co., 135 U. S. Inft.
Cartwright, Boyd.
Claveau, Lloyd, U. S. S. Kansas.
Caron, Octave, 151 U. S. F. A. Co., 76-0 A. E. F.
Claveau, Fred, First Field Bat. Co. B., A. E. F.
Carlson, Melvin, U. S. S. Iowa.
Clark, Matt, Med. Dept.
Christenson, John Oscar.
Cook, Chas., Co. B. 10th Eng., A. E. F.
Case, Russell, 40 Ballon Div.
Coathup, Russell, Coast Art.
Champoux, Edward, "Spruce Div."
Campbell, Irving Earl, Ordinance Dept.
Carlson, George O., Aviation Signal Corps.
Cash, William O.
Casey, Lieut. Roy E., Field Artillery.
Cox, Hanford, Ordinance Dept.
Chauklas, Donnis, 36th U. S. Inft.
Champoux, Henry.
Curtis, Wm. M., Honorable Discharge.
Carlson, Carl G. E., Coast Artillery.
Davidson, Wm. F., 32nd R. R. Engineers.
Davidson, J. R., A. E. F.
Douglas, Leslie.
Defoe, John.
Davis Trimble F., Y. M. C. A. War Work, A. E. F.
Dreschler, George, Co. 34 2nd Reg. C. A. M. A.
Demars Harry, 136 Hdq. Co.
Delyea, Will, "Spruce Div."
Drew, H. J., Co. C. 59 Inft.
Dulong, Corp. Henry, Co. I. First Bat. 107 Eng.
Delyea, Frank, Batt. F. 60th Reg. Coast Art.
Delarosby, Oscar, "Spruce Div."
Dugay, Raymond, "Spruce Div."
Desilets, Octave, 39 Co. C. A. N. A.
Desilets, Phil, Aviation Signal Corps.
Dennis, Isidore.
Dobrowiski, Ed., Honorable Discharge.
Deperry, Antonie.
Dunphy, Stephen.
Ervin, Fred, Co. I. 45th Inft.
Erickson, Edwin, U. S. S. Iowa.
Erickson, Howard L., "Spruce Div."
Esko, Chas.
Ervin, Frank.
Franklin, Louis, Batt. A. 17th F. A., A. E. F.
Fryklund, Verne, Honorable Disclarge.
Guittard, Lieut. V. D., M. R. C.
Gellerman, Floyd R., U. S. N. R. F. Radio School.
Grunig, Walter, Co. C. Hosp.
Graves, Sargt. William, 20th Eng., A. E. F.
Gilbreath, W. J., Batt. D. 135 Fld. Art.
Gilbreath, Zebben, Aviation Sig. Corps.
Glass, Fredrick.
Gray, Robert, "Spruce Div."
Gamble, Arthur, Co. B. 5th Fld. Batt. Sig. Corps.
Gilbert, Lieut. Leo, Co. H. 352 Inft.
Graton, Robert, 136 Inft. Hdq. Co.
Gerin, Louis G., Y. M. C. A.
Guinella, William.
Hostman, Gust Wm.
Haaerlin, Fred, Barracks No. 4 Co. 27.
Hackett, Emmett, Hospital Corps, 125 F. A.
Handran, Stephan, Troop E. 6th Cavalry.
Holmes, John Francis, "Spruce Div." Aviation Sec.
Huot, Oliver, Co. F. 8th B. M. 20th Eng., A. E. F.
Harney, Lieut. John J., Co. B. 127 Machine Gun Batt.
Harney, Thomas, 4th Batt. Co. I. U. S. Naval Training.
Harney, Malachi L., U. S. Marine Corps.
Halverson, Clifford, I. N. C. Utility Dept. Co. D. Barracks 1227.
Hawley, James, 61st Inft. 5 Div. Mach. Gun Co.
Hill, Curtis, 125 Reg. U. S. F. A. Co. A.
Hall, Carl F. R., Medical Dtch. 350 Inft.
Hansen, Ray M., Q. M. C.
Hobbs, Douglas.
Haines, Jack.
Hagen, Sivert.
Hall, Wm. E., Co. D. 10th Eng., A. E. F.
Hanson, Fritz, Co. A. 147 Mach. Gun, A. E. F.
Hautala, John W., Co. A. 46th Inft.
Hebert, Charles D., U. S. Naval Air Service, A. E. F.
Hackett, John.
Hanson, Ed. R., Batt. A. 17th F. A.
Hudberg, Erick, Aviation Sig. Corps.
Houl, Christi.
Horan, William, Coast Art.
Hervis, Arvid.
Honiemi, John.
John, Emanuel, U. S. S. Pubio.
Jubie, Alfred, "Spruce Div."
John, James, 116 Amn. Train, 1st Truck Co., A. E. F.
Johnson, Reid.
Jackson, Oscar G., 621st Aerial Squadron.
Johnson, Carl G., "Spruce Div."
Juotas, John Emil.
Johnson, Andrew, Co. I. 8th U. S. Inft.
Johnson, Nels.
Johnson, Henry, Co. L. 62nd Inft.
Johnson, Arthur L., 355 Inft. Co. Med. Dtch.
Johnson, Raynold, 125 U. S. Fld. Art. Hdqts.
Johnson, Geo. C., 125 Machine Gun. Batt. Co. B. 34th Div.
Johnson, J. M., Co. C. 7th Batt. Hdq. 20th Eng., A. E. F.
Johnson, Henry, Aviation Sig. Corps.
Johnson, Irving, Canadian Army.
Johnson, William A., U. S. Marine Corps.
Kinney, Myrton R., 4th Division.
Kinney, Ceylon G., Fld. Hosp. Med. Officer Dept. Co. 16.
Karjala, Isaac Wm.
Kempke, Wm. John, 20th Eng. Forestry Div.
Kayala, Emil A.
Kleckner, Fred.
Keller, Benedict O., Co. E. 4th Bat. 20th Eng., A. E. F.
Keonse, August, Prov. Amb. Co.
Kultu, Edurund, Coast Artillery.
Krzeloniski, Frank.
Kelseth, Geo., C. A. C. 13th Band Ft.
Krohn, Axel, 18 Inft., A. E. F.
Kellar, Lieut. Clarence, Camp Custer.
Kramer, Edward.
Kopp, Lewis M., Co. S. 5 Bn. 163 Depot Brig.
Loisel, Simon M., Co. A. 10th Eng. Forestry Div., A. E. F.
Levasseur, Fred, Batt. A. 17th F. A., A. E. F.
Longtin, Leo, 127 Mach. Bat. Co. B., 34th Div.
Levack, Alfred, Brigade Hdq. 66th Brig.
Lingren, Rudolph, "Spruce Div."
LeSavage, Henry, "Spruce Div."
LeBreche, Edwin, "Spruce Div."
LeBreche, Joseph, "Spruce Div."
Loisel, Joseph F., "Spruce Div." Aviation Sec.
LeMay, Edward J.
Loisel, Simond, "Spruce Div." Aviation Sec.
Leimer, Lieut. Ray, 1st Inft. Co.
LeBrasseur, John, Co. M. 358 Inft.
Lqee, Ernest, Honorable Discharge.
Leland, Signor.
LeBrasseur, Simon.
Laundry, Chas.
Lippke, Max.
Lundquist, Wm.
Laveau, Alex, Co. M. 358 Inft.
Lindquist, John E., Med. Dtch. 350th Inft.
Leonard, Paul, 20th Eng.
Laundry, Ed.
Larson, Hjalmar.
Lamirande, Earnest, "Spruce Div."
LaDroute, Geo., Co. H. 348 Inft.
LaDroute, Arthur, "Spruce Div."
La Londe, Alfred, Naval Base S. C. 2nd Class Cook.
Leimeux, Peter, A. E. F., France.
La Prairie, Louis, Co. A. 32nd Engineers.
Lahti, John, Coast Artillery.
La Fave, John.
LaBrasseur, Hector.
LeBlanc, Jos.
LeBreche, Elmer.
LaBlanc, Leo.
LaBlanc, Arthur.
Lessor, Archie, Co. E. 133 U. S. Inft.
Lamirande, Herbert, Medical Corps.
Mallory, Walter Herman, Co. M. 350 Inft.
McGillvary, Gordon, 405 Squadron A. A. S. C.
Mangum, Henry, 9th Co. C. A. C.
McNair, Lieut. C. I. Jr., Officers' Training Camp.
Metcalf, Leo.
McGrann, Geo. T.
McGough, Edmund P., 313 Eng. Co. D.
Martin, Arsene J., 133 Co. U. S. Marine Corps, A. E. F.
McCoubrey, Allan, Honorable Discharge.
McKale, William, "Spruce Div."
MacMillan, Donald, Co. B. 10th Eng., A. E. F.
McGillivray, Earl, Co. E. 10th Eng., A. E. F.
McClosky, Wilbert J., Co. 5, U. S. Marines, A. E. F.
Mannu, John F.
McWithey, Harry.
MacMillan, Roy.
McGuire, Ernest M., Co. 5, Marine Barracks.
McCarthy, Emmett, Aviation Sec. Sig. Corp.
McClay, Edgar.
Martin, William, Co. K. 61st Inft. 5th Div.
McDonnell, James G., Brigade Hdq. 66th Brigade.
McCluskey, James R., Q. M. C., N. R. S. No. 303, A. E. F.
Mitchell, Alfred, "Spruce Div."
Moski, Peter, "Spruce Div."
Marttinen, Nestor.
McGugin, John, Canadian Army.
McTague, Leonard.
Michaelson, Victor J.
Markowitz, Max, Aviation Sig. Corps.
Moody, John R.
McKenna, Fred.
Murray, Laurence, Honorable Discharge.
Morken, Ole, Honorable Discharge.
Meagher, Thomas, Depot Co. I. Signal Corp.
Nygard, Leif.
Nelson, Adolph, 25th Co. 2nd Reg. C. A. C. M. A.
Nelson, Walter T., Co. S. 163 Depot Brigade.
Narkowski, Louis.
Nehiba, Arnold.
Nielson, Nikolai.
Norman, George, M. M. 2 Cl. U. S. S. North Carolina.
Nygren, William.
Nichols, Lieut. Geo. E., Camp Custer.
Ornell, Carl G., "Spruce Div."
O'Neil, W. J., 3rd Batt. O. T. C. Barracks 42.
O'Neil, E. H.
O'Hearn, Frank, France.
O'Hearn, Joseph, 34 Comp. 2 C. A. C. N. A.
Oswald, John, 33rd Inft., A. E. F.
Olson, Sergt. Oliver W.
Oswald, Knute.
Olin, Walter, Co. B. 125th Machine Gun Bat.
Owens, Harry, Brigade Hdq. 66th Brigade.
Olson, John, Co. K. 46th Inft.
O'Hearn, Irving D., 54th Co. 2nd Reg. 1st Brigade, U. S. Marines.
O'Brien, John Frederick.
O'Neil, Daniel, 125th Fld. Art.
Olson, Louis L., Honorable Discharge.
O'Mara, Walter, Coast Artillery.
Poirier, Corp. Ray, Co. I. 45th Inft.
Poquette, Clarence E., "Spruce Div."
Powell, Garnet C., Kelly Field.
Peterson, John B.
Perry, Charles, 1st Minn. Fld. Art. Batt. B.
Patterson, Wm. E., Co. D.
Pengttila, Penparte M., 350 Prov. Amb. Co.
Pera, Oscar L.
Prudhom, Angus.
Peterson, Elmer M., Co. C. 42nd Inft.
Peters, Sergt. Lester, Co. A. 147 Mach. Gun Co., A. E. F.
Potterud, Marshall, Co. C. 5th Eng.
Provost, Samuel G., Co. E. 352nd Inft.
Pappio, J. A., U. S. S. Castine.
Peacha, Francis B., "Spruce Div."
Pollard, Marvin, Railroad Eng. Corps.
Perry, Frank, Aviation Sig. Corps.
Proulx, George A.
Quinn, Edward, 429th Aero Squad. Const. Sqd.
Racette, Edmund F., Field No. 2 Hempsted.
Rodgers, Wm., Co. D. 10th Eng., A. E. F.
Redfield, Frank, Bat. C. 125 U. S. Art.
Rodgers, Walter, Co. A. 3rd Minn. Reg.
Rogers, Chas. B., Co. 3 337 M. G. Br.
Rogentine, John, 40th Co. 2nd Prov. Reg.
Richter, Arthur, Co. B. 125 Mach. Gun Bat.
Ripplinger, Carl.
Rousseau, Sergt. Eugene, Co. B. 10th Eng., A. E. F.
Raiter, Lieut. Franklin, Amt. Co. 136.
Roy, Jos. O., Batt. F. 17th Fld. Art., A. E. F.
Rabideau, Orville, "Spruce Div."
Rice, Thomas, "Spruce Oiv."
Randa, Hugo Arthur.
Raski, John.
Skagerberg, Rutcher, Flying Cadet Squadron.
Smith, Walter A., 69th Co. U. S. Marines.
Santere, Lieut. Frank, Batt. M-6 Prov. C. A. C., A. E. F.
Sparen, E. H., Honorable Discharge.
Sunnarborg, Benjamin W., 48 Machine Gun Co.
Sota, Dr. John, Honorable Discharge.
Sahlman, Waino W., Honorable Discharge.
Stevens, D. E., U. S. N. Aviation Corps, A. E. F.
Sandstrom, Randolph.
Sapenokis, Dionicis, 36th Inft. U. S. A.
Sorensen, Alvin, Co. D. 36th Reg. Inft.
Sand, Thomas.
Soulier, Willie.
Salmela, Arthur L.
Swerz, Stoini.
Shaffer, Frank.
Smith, Corp. F. W.
Seikkula, Niilo.
Sheean, Lyman, Honorable Discharge.
Stevens, W. H., Brigade Hdq. 66th Brig.
Stevens, Lieut. Geo. A., 316 Reg.
Swenson, Einer M., Co. I 42nd Inft.
Swenson, Reuben A., died in the service.
Starrs, John L., Co. F. 4th Bat. 20th Eng., A. E. F.
Serre, A. H., Motor Amb. Co. 19 M. O. T. C.
Summerfield, Wm., Batt. A. 62nd Reg. C. A. C. N. A.
Sandstrom, C. L., Y. M. C. A.
Skagerberg, Elon, Aviation Sig. Corps.
Swanson, John, Aviation Sig. Corps.
Swanson, Andrew W.
Sather, Emil.
Tobin, Lieut. Paul.
Thompson, Gilbert, Medical Dept. Amb. Co. 17.
Tonkin, Albert.
Ultican, John.
Underhill, James K., Sanitary Squad No. 2 A. T. O. 127, A. E. F.
Vnuk, Leo J., 59 Inf. Med. Corps.
Vnuk, John.
Vibert, Roland, 20th Eng. 6th Batt. Co. F., A. E. F.
Vibert, Reginald, Co. E. 10th Eng., A. E. F.
Wagner, Joe, M. G. Co. 136 Inft.
Williams, Rev. W. E., Y. M. C. A.
White, Ira D.
Wood, Laurence, Co. K. 45th Inft.
Woods, Miles, 314 Sanitary Tr. Prov. Fld. Hosp. Co. C.
Westerberg, Carl, Co. D. 20th Eng., A. E. F.
Wagner, John, Co. E. 408 Telegraph Barracks, A. E. F.
Wiggin, G. H., Co. E. 6th Batt. 20th Eng., A. E. F.
Wight, Lloyd, Co. F. 313th Supply Tr.
White, Elmer Leon, "Spruce Div."
Wodny, Stanley, Carnegie Inst.
Williams, Charles H.
Wilson, Leslie, Canadian Army.
Whitman, Mark.
Westman, John E.
Youngbauer, Wm., Co. M. 350th Inft.
Yager, V. J., Co. 10 Detention Camp.
Young, Geo. A., U. S. S. Kansas.
Yetka, Frank, Co. B. 34th Eng., A. E. F.
Younge, William Jr., Co. I 127 Inft., A. E. F.
Zellerberg, Algot E.
Zankoski, Peter.

legislation for the national prohibition of spirituous liquors. Prohibitionist sentiment had existed from the very founding of the village of Cloquet and was also strongly felt in the surrounding townships. The city even boasted a temperance society and fellowship hall in the years before 1918.

When this "List of Cloquet Boys Serving in the United States Army and Navy" was published, readers were asked to report any errors or missing names to ensure an accurate record.

Added to the social concerns was a growing feeling of unrest in the country over the agitation of unions and groups sympathetic to workers for better working conditions. Communists, socialists, and other groups advocating radical or even moderate social change were especially suspect. Suspicion of the foreign born, particularly those from countries at war with the United States, was widespread during World War I. These feelings continued after the war and were expressed in various ways, both locally and nationally.

TWO CLOQUET DIS-LOYALISTS MOBBED

ONE WAS TARRED AND FEATHERED AND OTHER WHIPPED.

BY THE KNIGHTS OF LIBERTY

UNQUESTIONABLY AN ORGANIZATION EXISTS TO HANDLE DISLOYAL CASES.

Newspaper articles during the First World War frequently contained articles about loyalty. The March 29, 1918, edition of the *Carlton County Vidette* contained a story about two Cloquet "disloyalists" who were mobbed by a group of masked men who called themselves the "Knights of Liberty." Otto Lehne, the night ticket agent at the Cloquet depot, was tarred and feathered. The Knights also reportedly took George Sahlman, a prominent resident of Cloquet, out of town and administered a sound beating for alleged pro-German statements. A popular account about Sahlman differs substantially from the news clipping. He was supposedly rescued in the nick of time by a group of friends from the Toivola Company, who then dispersed the Knights.

During the fall of 1918, world and national events changed drastically. Fall also brought with it a catastrophe that forever changed the city of Cloquet. On Saturday, October 12th, the community was largely destroyed by a firestorm of epic proportions. The event was so completely devastating that it has remained a defining moment in the lives of some of Cloquet's citizens to this very day. Although the forest fire that destroyed Cloquet was one of several fires that occurred throughout the area, it was invariably referred to by some who survived it as "the fire." For years thereafter, events were described as happening " before the fire" or "after the fire."

Perhaps the most dramatic event that ever occurred in Cloquet was the catastrophic forest fire of 1918 that completely destroyed the town. The scope of the disaster can be appreciated when one looks at a map of the city of Cloquet just before the fire. With few exceptions, everything on the south side of the railroad tracks burned.

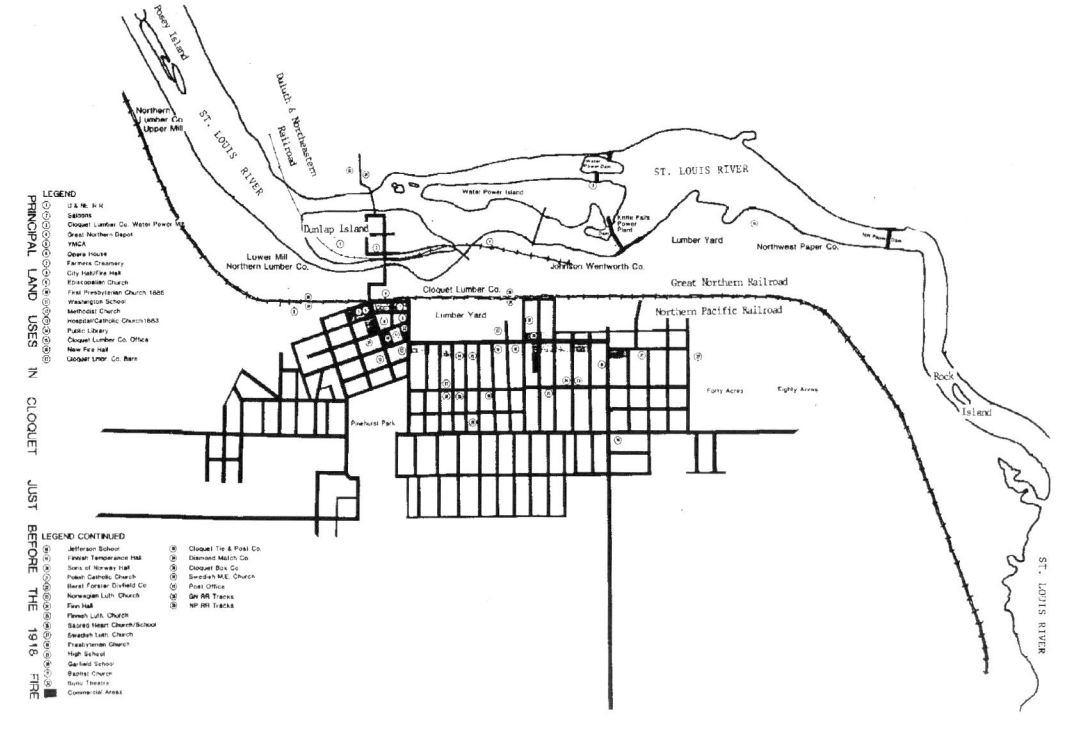

To date, a great deal has been written about the forest fires of 1918. Perhaps some of the interest in the story of the fires which swept through much of Carlton and adjoining counties, has been inspired by the long-term effect the disaster had on the region and on Cloquet in particular.

Most histories of the 1918 disaster agree that the fire which destroyed Cloquet started near milepost 62 on the Great Northern Railroad and was aided by natural conditions which caused the fire to create its own draft as it moved through the forest. By the afternoon of October 12th, the fire was moving in a general southeasterly direction toward the St. Louis River valley.

As the blaze progressed, it destroyed the town of Brookston and many farms in its path. Local residents were forced to flee, and many refugees departed for Cloquet by train. In the process, they ran a gauntlet of fire which burned along both sides of the railroad tracks.

While gaining in intensity, the fire entered the Fond du Lac Indian Reservation and destroyed many homes there. All day the sun shone red through the smokey atmosphere as ashes rained down on Cloquet. Toward evening, the glow of the approaching fire could be seen through thick rolling clouds of smoke while the wind created by the holocaust steadily increased. The community with its five sawmills, paper mill and related industries, along with homes and small businesses, stood directly in its path.

The story of the evacuation of Cloquet before the onrushing firestorm has often emphasized the role of the railroad in providing the means of escape. While it is true that many residents left by train, many also traveled by automobile, wagon, or simply walked. Some chose to stay. Others left the town only to return while it was still burning to see if there was anything they could save.

Efforts were made to save the community when the fire first entered the town near the Northern Lumber Company's upper mill. The city fire department tried to extinguish blazes as they broke out, but the scope of the fire was too great and they pulled back. It was said the force of the wind was so strong it blew the spray from the fire hoses back in the men's faces. An attempt was also made by mill owners and workers to save sawmill property; and to a certain extent, their efforts were successful.

When morning came, the full extent of the disaster quickly became apparent. Gone were two of the five sawmills, the post and tie company, and many other structures. Miraculously, most of the town's industrial base remained intact. The big question facing everyone was whether or not to rebuild. Most of the mills had survived, but the vast majority of the freshly sawn timber was destroyed as were most of the homes of the people who worked in those mills.

The scene of devastation that greeted many who fled from the flames. One of the only structures to survive the fire was the water tower.

Photo by Olaf Olson

Cloquet's rise from the ashes of October 12, 1918, has been compared to that of the mythical phoenix. An outpouring of relief for the homeless came in many forms and from many sources. Food, clothing, medicine, medical assistance, and free materials with which to build temporary standardized shelters, later dubbed "fire shacks," were made available. Countless residents who had fled before the advancing flames were sheltered and fed in private homes in surrounding communities such as Carlton and Duluth, Minnesota, and Superior, Wisconsin.

As if to compound the disaster, the Spanish Influenza pandemic threatened to spread into the fire area. Strict quarantine measures, enforced by contingents of the Minnesota Home Guard, were quickly put in place to halt the spread of disease and prevent unauthorized people from entering the disaster area. Order was maintained in the fire district and the ravages of the Spanish Influenza were limited largely because of the quarantine.

In the weeks and months following the October 12th disaster, the heartening renaissance of Cloquet occurred as more and more of the residents were encouraged to commit themselves to rebuilding their city. It was, however, a city that could no longer look back on its fame as a sawmilling center. Even if the fire had never occurred, circumstances were already at work in 1918 that led to the reshaping of the timber industry, so long a mainstay of the local economy. No longer could the timber industry be thought of solely in terms of the number of board feet of lumber produced.

The economic and social changes wrought by the events of World War I and the Great Fire of 1918 were partially obscured by the national prosperity that followed during the 1920s. There still remained, however, one serious issue for many of Cloquet's residents. That issue concerned the indemnification by the government for fire losses. It was an issue that remained unresolved until well into the 1930s.

The post-war prosperity proved to be both unparalleled in the history of the country and short lived. In

Where once a busy sawmill stood, only the charred ruins of a few buildings and the refuse burner remain. Both of the Northern Lumber Company's mills burned on October 12, 1918. After the fire, only the company's lower mill was rebuilt.

Photo by Olaf Olson

October of 1929, the stock market crashed, and the events that followed precipitated the Great Depression of the 1930s. Despite a continued bleak economic outlook for the country, Cloquet never felt the full impact of the depression compared to many other communities. Thanks in part to new industries which grew up following the destruction of the town, there were always some jobs available, even though at the time, work was scarce.

The long stagnant period known as the Great Depression was finally brought to a close by the outbreak of the Second World War. Once again, the United States became "the arsenal of democracy" for the rest of the world as Cloquet's citizens and products were called into war service.

The half century following the period of the Great Depression and World War II, saw great changes in lifestyle, as well as in the lives of the citizens of Cloquet. The fact that the town managed to weather two world wars, a disastrous fire, and the worst economic depression ever experienced, and still survive is a remarkable testament to the endurance and fortitude of the citizens of Cloquet. It is a story worth remembering.

In this scene, workmen are busy demolishing the remaining walls of a burned-out building so that reconstruction can begin on the site.

The work of reconstruction began almost as soon as the flames subsided. Here workmen are cleaning debris and beginning work on the new Cloquet Auto & Supply Company.

Amid the destruction, one can see the beginning of reconstruction. In the center of the photograph are shown a new home, a temporary tent shelter, and next to the tent, a fire shack. In the lower right side of the picture, workmen are busy roofing a house.

An example of the reconstruction in the business district along Avenue C after the fire. Note the ubiquitous water tower behind the new buildings. Within a decade, most of the old neighborhoods of Cloquet were rebuilt.

Workmen hurry to finish framing a new two story home in Cloquet even as snow begins to pile up by the front steps. Many homes with this general floor plan were constructed immediately after the Fire of 1918.

A photograph of a typical fire shack as it appeared in 2003. Many of these temporary relief shelters were converted to garages or storage sheds. Some are still used as dwellings in the community.

Photo by Marlene Wisuri

107

While news of major world events made front page headlines, other catastrophes occurred which attracted the attention of Cloquet's residents. In 1916, the St. Louis River rose over its banks and flooded Dunlap Island and the Northern Lumber Company's lower mill as shown here.

On May 6, 1950, the St. Louis River once again rose over its banks and flooded Dunlap Island and the surrounding area. This time the rushing water caused extensive damage when it tore out the Duluth & Northeastern Railroad Company's bridge. The scene here shows the flood damage on the north side of Dunlap Island.

Fires were a common occurrence in a city built of wood. This picture shows all that remains of the Johnson Mercantile Company after a disastrous fire in 1912.

The occasional spectacular fire could draw large crowds. This dramatic photograph shows the fire ball from an exploding fuel storage tank during a bulk plant fire on April 1, 1943. Two railroad employees were killed as a result of the blast as they attempted to move nearby railroad cars away from the fire.

Other types of tragedies, such as the first serious flying mishap in Minnesota, also made headlines. The March 25th, 1921, edition of the *Pine Knot*, tells the fascinating story of the crash which took place near Cloquet in a blinding snow storm. The plane's occupants were seriously injured in the accident.
Photo by Harold F. Gillaspy

In the years between World War I and World War II, Cloquet's residents not only rebuilt the town, but also the industrial base. Shown here is a dedication ceremony for the new flag pole at the Wood Conversion Company in 1927. All of the company's employees were present for the event.

In spite of economic woes, patriotism remained strong. Veterans' organizations participated in various community celebrations. The Carl Anderson American Legion Post Drum and Bugle Corps poses in front of the post home at Seventh Street and Carlton Avenue in 1933.

Photo by Olaf Olson

The stock market crash of 1929 and the onset of the Great Depression came scarcely a decade after the Fire of 1918, but Cloquet was able to withstand the challenge. Relief measures enacted to combat the economic depression included the establishment of the Civilian Conservation Corps (CCC). The photograph above, taken on May 29, 1934, shows part of the Big Lake CCC Camp S-79.

Photo by G.O. Mehl

The building of the St. Louis River viaduct was the largest public works project undertaken in Cloquet during the Great Depression. It replaced two older bridges, and according to one account, it gave "the central section of the community an impressive appearance."

Another major project was the building of the Cloquet Post Office in 1935. The money and jobs generated by these projects helped ease the dreadful impact of the depression on the community.

111

Cloquet's residents faced new restrictions when the United States entered World War II in December of 1941. The ration coupon book shown here became a part of the everyday routine for the duration of the conflict.

Local industries reminded their employees to be as efficient as possible in furthering the war effort.
Northwest Paper Company distributed these note pads to employees and customers in 1944.

The effect of the war on the home front could be seen in every industry. Women filled many vital roles. This scene of an office Christmas party for the staff of the Personnel Department of the Northwest Paper Company, is dominated by women. Personnel Manager Arthur C. Dobrowolski (seated) and Lawrence Cardinal, in the upper right-hand corner, are the only men present.

Parades and celebrations were used in an effort to boost morale and stimulate public support of the war effort. The parade float shown in this 1942 photograph, sponsored by the Cloquet Co-op, urged citizens to buy war bonds.

Gasoline was tightly rationed. Most vehicle owners were limited to a basic mileage ration or "A" card similar to the one shown here.

Everyone had to get into the act. During the war, youngsters often dressed up as soldiers and sailors. Children's military attire was not merely a fashion statement, but a genuine expression of support for the men and women in the armed services.

Pictured on the left is six year old Ricard Puumala looking very soldierly. On the right are two "gobs" ready to take on the enemy. Larry Luukkonen and his father, Arnold M. Luukkonen, pose in their navy dress blues.

113

Francis John "Cheech" Godfrey of the U.S. Army Air Force gives the "V" for victory sign.

Newspaper stories kept people apprised of the war.

Cloquet Marine is Decorated By Admiral Nimitz in Hospital

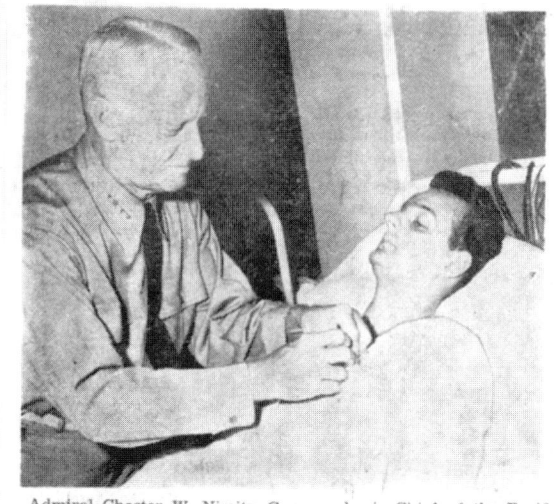

Admiral Chester W. Nimitz, Commander-in-Chief of the Pacific Ocean area, recently paid a personal visit to the bedside of Marine Private First Class Elwood J. Ferguson, of Cloquet, and pinned the Order of the Purple Heart medal on his chest. Private First Class Ferguson was wounded shortly after he landed on the beach at Saipan Island.

Pictures sent to the folks at home helped boost morale.

Beatrice Yanda of Cloquet posed for a picture in her dress uniform while serving as a nurse in London in 1943.

IN MEMORIAM

DEDICATED by The Northwest Paper Company in reverent tribute to the memory of those from its organization who gave their lives in the Armed Services of our Country during the Second World War.

They died that we may continue to follow our American way of life. May their souls rest in eternal peace and may loving memory of them reside in our hearts forever.

Sincerely,

Stuart R. Copeland
PRESIDENT

May 30, 1946

Some of those who went off to war did not return. The sentiments expressed in this memorial, published by the Northwest Paper Company, reflect the deep appreciation felt by many for the sacrifices of the members of the armed services during the war.

William H. Dupont graduated from Cloquet High School in 1935. He was a bomber pilot in the Army Air Corps and was killed in action in Europe on September 26, 1944.

A color guard, made up of members of local veterans' organizations, leads a parade through Pinehurst Park. During and after World War II sizable contingents of veterans graced every holiday parade.

A parade float on Carlton Avenue at Eleventh Street in the 1940s, sponsored by American Legion Post 262, reminds the audience of what can happen "Lest we forget."

The 1950s saw service men from Cloquet once again involved in a military conflict. Anthony F. Jurek entered the army in August, 1949, at the age of seventeen. He was sent to Korea in 1950 and became a North Korean Prisoner of War on December 1, 1950. He was imprisoned until August, 1953. He often speaks to school groups about his experiences as a POW.

Another generation of Cloquet residents served during the Vietnam War. This photo was taken of Lance Corporal Scott Belfry, U.S. Marine Corps, somewhere in the Queson Mountains, Republic of South Vietnam, in February, 1971.

In 2003, the United States was involved in yet another military conflict—Operation Iraqi Freedom. Nathan Pollak, valedictorian of his 1996 Cloquet High School class, entered the Marine Corps upon his graduation from Duke University. He served in the First Expeditionary Force of the Marines in Iraq where he is pictured in a bunker in the spring of 2003.

Photo courtesy of Brenda Pollak

Cloquet's first female West Point Millitary Academy graduate, Teresa Smith Pleinis, graduated at the top of her Cloquet High School class in 1990. She is pictured above in her Millitary Academy graduation photograph in 1994. Major Pleinis has served in Haiti, Hawaii, and several other stateside locations and is currently a finance officer at Fort Bragg, North Carolina. Among her many awards is the General Douglas MacArthur Leadership Award.

Photo courtesy of Renee Smith

The dedication of a monument honoring veterans of all the wars took place on July 14, 2000, at Veterans' Memorial Park on the Fond du Lac Reservation.

Photo by Marlene Wisuri

This aerial view of Cloquet, taken about 1955, shows few signs of former sawmill operations. Only the refuse burner of the Northern Lumber Company's mill is still operating and even that structure, shown here emitting a wispy cloud of smoke, soon vanished. The new D & NE railroad bridge, which replaced the one destroyed by the flood in 1950, stands a few hundred feet downstream from the old bridgehead. The Wood Conversion Company's plant, in the center of the picture, dwarfs the old sawmills that once operated along the St. Louis River, and is typical of the new businesses that arose to take their place.

Chapter Six
A Resilient Community

One of the enduring characteristics of Cloquet is its resilience. Influenced by its location, sustained by the residents of the community, tested by the rigors of war, disaster, and depression, the city and its economy have grown steadily. Looking back through the community's history, one can trace certain elements and conditions which greatly favored the development of the local economy.

Initially, the geographical location of the community and available transportation were two very important factors that influenced the business vitality of Cloquet. These factors were present when the community was founded and are still very important today. In addition, the water resources of the St. Louis River, first used for transportation, were later harnessed in the twentieth century for the production of electricity. Also, the advent of a modern highway system was crucial to the development of the industrial base of the community.

Likewise, the products of the forest have served as the mainstay of the community from its formative years to the present day. In the one hundred years since Cloquet was first organized as a city, wood, whether in the form of lumber or as specialty products, has always played a major role in the economy.

One test of the adaptability of Cloquet's economy came at the height of its glory as a traditional sawmill center. By the end of the first decade of the twentieth century, it was clear to most mill owners that the supply of large marketable white pine would soon run out. For years the harvest of mature timber had been the main focus of the industry. There remained, however, thousands of acres of young second-growth timber, including what some termed "waste wood" or "weed trees."

> ...the products of the forest have served as the mainstay of the community from its formative years to the present day.

The question was how to make use of the remaining resources. Fortunately, manufacturers had begun to look at trees increasingly as a source of fiber and not necessarily simply as lumber. Early on, the mill owners in Cloquet saw in the manufacture of paper one answer to the question of how best to utilize the existing forest resources. In 1898, the Northwest Paper Company's paper mill was established in Cloquet and began the production of ground pulp for the manufacture of newsprint. From that small beginning emerged the present modern mill operated by Sappi Fine Papers.

The construction of the new Northwest Paper Company mill, shown here in 1898, marked the beginning of the transformation of Cloquet's economy. Note the tramway and horses used in the construction work. Much of the heavy work was still done by hand and horse power.

Other new uses for wood as specialty products, such as the manufacture of wooden shipping containers, were quickly developed. The Berst Company began the manufacture of clothespins and other specialty products in its Cloquet mill in 1905. Later, reorganized as the Berst-Forster-Dixfield Company, the firm added wooden matches to its product line. Some of these products continued to be manufactured by its successor, the Diamond Match Company. It was, however, in the use of wood as a source of fiber that Cloquet excelled. In fact, a specific company was organized to look into the development of useful products utilizing wood fiber.

The creation of the Wood Conversion Company shortly after the disastrous fire of 1918 opened up a whole new market for second-growth timber which flourished in the burned over region. The company produced insulation and a type of wood composition board.

These products, known as "Balsam-Wool" and "Nu-wood," filled an important market niche and were staple products for many decades. Other products were added later, such as acoustical ceiling tile and cushioning material.

The Diamond Match Company (formerly Berst-Forster-Dixfield) manufactured wooden matches and other specialty products. It utilized birch, which like aspen, was considered a "weed tree." The white building in the foreground was the plant office.

Companies such as the Northwest Paper Company, the Berst-Forster-Dixfield Company, and the Wood Conversion Company started the transition of Cloquet from a sawmill town to a more diversified wood products center. Meanwhile, Cloquet's economy has also become increasingly diversified over the years and therein lies another secret of its resiliency.

The many service industries that first grew up to provide for the needs of the sawmills and logging companies also offered their services to new local businesses. The new industries played an important role, and many continued in business long after their old sawmill clientele ceased operation in the 1930s. One important example involved the generation of electricity—first for the sawmills, then for the community, and finally for the surrounding area.

While the focus of Cloquet's economy turned increasingly away from the traditional logging and sawmill industries situated along the river front, an old and very important source of energy associated with one of those sawmills, the Water Power Company, was tapped in the 1920s. The General Light and Power Company constructed a hydroelectric station in Cloquet on the historic site of the Knife Falls. It was one of several built to harness the power of the St. Louis River. Early in its history, Cloquet's source of electric power was limited.

It was generated by a small steam plant before the Knife Falls station was built. The electricity it produced was used chiefly by the sawmills. The large new hydroelectric facility built at the Knife Falls foreshadowed the important growth in the energy business and its positive impact on the community and region in the years to come.

The hydroelectric dams on the St. Louis River are unique, for they use the flow of the river through the turbines five times to generate electricity. The Northwest Paper Company also generated electricity from both its hydroelectric facilities and from steam produced in operating the mill. Surplus electricity, when available, was sold to the electric company. The availability of inexpensive and plentiful electric power was an important factor in the future growth of business in Cloquet.

In addition to service and allied industries, a large number of family-owned businesses continued to supply needed goods and services, regardless of the fate of the big sawmills. Main street businesses and neighborhood stores have certainly contributed their share to the health of the local economy during the past century. These businesses survived the passing of the sawmill era because they were able to adapt to accommodate different tastes and needs of the community. Their very resiliency has enabled them to survive in prosperity and in recession. Family-

The General Light and Power Company's new hydroelectric station, shown in this 1923 photograph, harnessed the power of Knife Falls. Electricity produced by this plant, not only benefitted the residents and businesses of Cloquet, but also surrounding communities such as Scanlon, Carlton, Esko, Brookston, and Floodwood. The generating plant was electrically interconnected with other dams on the St. Louis River.

Photo by Olaf Olson from the collection of the Minnesota Historical Society

The Cloquet Creamery, located at 101 Avenue B, was an example of an early family owned business. It employed a number of local people and processed the products of area dairy farmers. The creamery was owned and operated for many years by brothers Oliver and LeBeau Huot.

Photo courtesy of Phyllis Markley

owned businesses still provide the essential core of Cloquet's economy.

Presently Cloquet's economy is marked by a very diversified blend of businesses, including the traditional wood industries; new industries like U.S. Gypsum, which manufactures construction products; large wholesale distributing businesses, such as oil companies and Upper Lakes Foods, which supplies restaurants throughout the region; and a modern shopping mall with a variety of stores, specialty shops, and offices.

The various building trades are well represented by a broad spectrum of local companies. Modern construction companies, such as Oscar J. Boldt Construction and Ray Riihiluoma Inc., contribute to the local economy as do a number of specialized contractors. Also, major retail outlets have recently expanded their facilities including L & M Supply and the new Wal-Mart Super Center.

Added to the list of businesses that make up the backbone of the local economy are those associated with the Fond du Lac Reservation. The development of the gaming industry on the reservation, construction of a first-class hotel facility, and the recent opening of a large golf course are only a few examples of new activities that have made the Fond du Lac Reservation the largest single employer in both the city of Cloquet and in Carlton County.

These are only some of the many factors that have helped make Cloquet's economy so adaptable. If one adds to the many businesses, the human resource provided by a diverse and educated populace, the strength of civic institutions and social organizations, the various amenities provided by the community, and the willingness to persevere in the face of adversity, then one has the recipe for the resiliency that has so typified the community for the past century.

The Cloquet Animal Hospital at 122 Second Street, is one example of the many types of service businesses which have contributed to Cloquet's economy and quality of life.

Photo by David Petite

Cloquet has progressed through one hundred years from a community essentially dependent upon the limited use of a single resource, to one which diversified and now looks beyond lumber production. Today the economy utilizes many different resources both natural and human.

We would do well to remember though, for everything gained something else is lost. For example, it is a paradox that as the city of Cloquet has grown over the years, the original name of the site—Knife Falls—has gradually been forgotten. From small beginnings on the banks of the St. Louis River an infant community grew to become a respectable city in its own right. In time, the city of Cloquet and township of Knife Falls merged.

Today, only the name Knife Falls remains to remind us of a former time when travelers paused at the head of *Le Portage des Couteaux* to reflect on what they had experienced. Their weary journey up the St. Louis River had brought them this far, but what lay ahead? So too may we pause after negotiating our way through this first century to reflect on where events may lead us in the next one hundred years. Hopefully, we will do as well as our predecessors.

Another Cloquet industry that utilized forest products was the Rathbone, Hair & Ridgway Company, commonly known as the "Box Factory." This plant made wooden boxes and box shooks. Shown here are the employees posing for a group picture in front of the plant in 1925. The standard work "uniform" of the women appears to have been knickers.   Photo is a detail of a panoramic photograph.

At first logging railroads made an easy transition from hauling saw logs to transporting pulp logs. In this posed picture, two managers at Northwest Paper gesture imaginatively as two workers slide logs into place with their pickaroons. Off to the side, a steam crane lifts logs from the bed of D&NE flatcars to a large stack to await processing into pulp.

Photo from the collection of the Miinnesota Historical Society, c. 1929

The railroad flatcars loaded with pulp logs shown in the background, were soon supplemented by trucks bringing loads of logs fresh from the woods to the mill. In this scene, a man is measuring the load of peeled pulp logs with a scale stick to determine the volume of the load.

This picture taken inside the Northwest Paper Company mill about 1929, shows a man about to cut a ream of paper to a desired size. Note the distinctive papermaker's hat. The square hat, made of folded paper, was the traditional badge of a craftsman. At the beginning of each shift the worker would cut and fold a new hat to protect his hair from the dust.

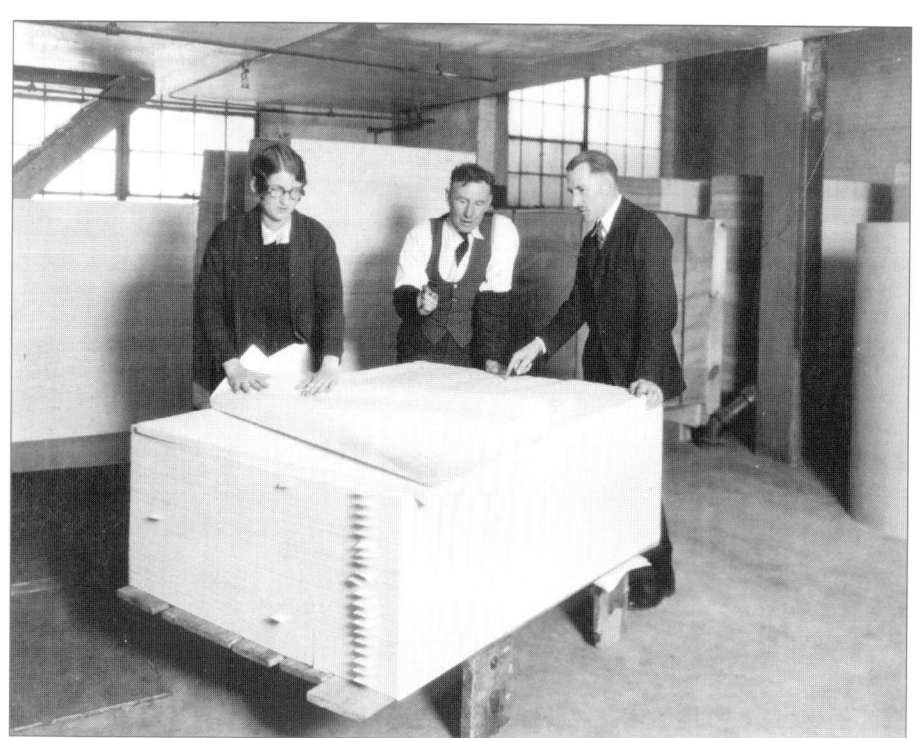

In this scene, also taken inside the paper mill about 1929, Clarabelle Franklin is "fanning" paper by the ream to check for defects while Thomas J. Crotty and C. I. McNair, Jr. look on. Note the sleeve protectors worn by Mr. Crotty to keep his shirt sleeves clean. Each stub of paper, or "fanner's ticket," protruding from the pile represents a ream of 500 sheets of paper.

Photos from the collection of the Minnesota Historical Society

These men are unloading aspen logs from flatcars at the Wood Conversion Company. Aside from paper, the first product made of wood fiber was "Balsam-Wool." It was "the original blanket insulation" and was followed by "Nu-Wood" in 1925.

A group of plant employees of the Wood Conversion Company pose with the first carload of Nu-wood shipped from Cloquet in 1925. Pictured from left to right, in front: E. S. Streator, Jalmar M. Larson, Theodore Daigle, Leonard R. Larson, middle row: Adolph Reed, Ivar Lund, E. Reed, Joseph Dean, in back: A. F. Jenkins, Harry Demers, E. Chounard, O. W. Frost, Charles Maynard, Unknown, Daniel S. Ridlington, J. William Nelson, Robert W. Ridlington, Myron Larson.

It seems as though some people will go to any length to sell their products. These two gnomes, clad in Balsam-Wool rolls and tights, pose in front of the company office in Cloquet.

Other innovative products were produced by the Wood Conversion Company such as "Tufflex," a new type of blanket insulation. The finished product of the Tufflex operation is shown in this photograph as it is being wound into rolls for shipping.

The Wood Conversion Company had its own fleet of trucks, emblazoned with advertising, to transport the company's products to nearby towns.

Retail stores also flourished in Cloquet. Shown here is the interior of the Baumann-Nesthus Men's Store in 1911. Note the shelves filled with shoe boxes on the left side of the photograph. The cylindrical boxes shown on top of the shelves are hat boxes. In the background is a full-length mirror where the well-dressed man-about-town could savor his sartorial splendor. Three piece men's suits were popular and normally included a vest, a coat, and two pair of trousers with watch pockets, something unheard of today.

Several new business ventures, such as the Trainer Aircraft Company, were started in Cloquet. The aircraft company, incorporated in 1931, manufactured a total of two prototype planes. Although the design of the planes was sound, it was difficult to raise adequate capital for mass production during the Great Depression. Unlike the planes, the company never really got off the ground.

Another short-lived business that began in Cloquet was the G. & W. Refrigerator Company. The company's plant was located in a two story building on the northeast corner of Twelfth Street and Cloquet Avenue. For a brief time, the Trainer Aircraft Company was located on the second floor of this building. How the airplane manufacturer ever got the planes out of the second story is unknown.

Some family owned businesses in Cloquet have operated for many decades. One example is Buskala's Jewelry Store which is one of the earliest Cloquet businesses. This 1923 photograph shows the interior of the jewelry store at 1010 Cloquet Avenue. Emil Buskala and Art Rautio are standing on the right side. The man on the left wearing a hat is a shirt salesman named Mr. Trevors.

This photograph shows the modern interior of Buskala's Jewelry Store with third generation owners, Joanne and John Buskala. The store has been expanded to include a line of gift items.

Photo by Timothy J. Krohn

Shown here is the Olsen Shoe Shop in 1953. It was a place where shoes could be repaired or purchased and is an example of the many small shops and services that thrived in Cloquet. On the left is Herman Olsen, shop owner, and Ray Luke is pictured on the right.

Restaurants have also been essential businesses throughout Cloquet's history. This early photograph shows the restaurant in the Wright Apartments building in the West End. The well-dressed clientele appear to be enjoying their meal, while the staff stand nearby ready to cater to their needs. The only person identified in this picture is Mae Laaksonen who is standing in the background, in front of the coffee urn.

Several of Cloquet's early saloons, such as the Moose Saloon on Dunlap Island, also featured separate restaurant facilities. Saloon bar rooms usually featured sandwiches, cold cuts, cheese and other delicacies to accompany the various beverages consumed by the patrons.

Saloon patrons stepped up to the ornately carved wooden bar which was characteristic of the times. The third man from the left is Joseph Caza.

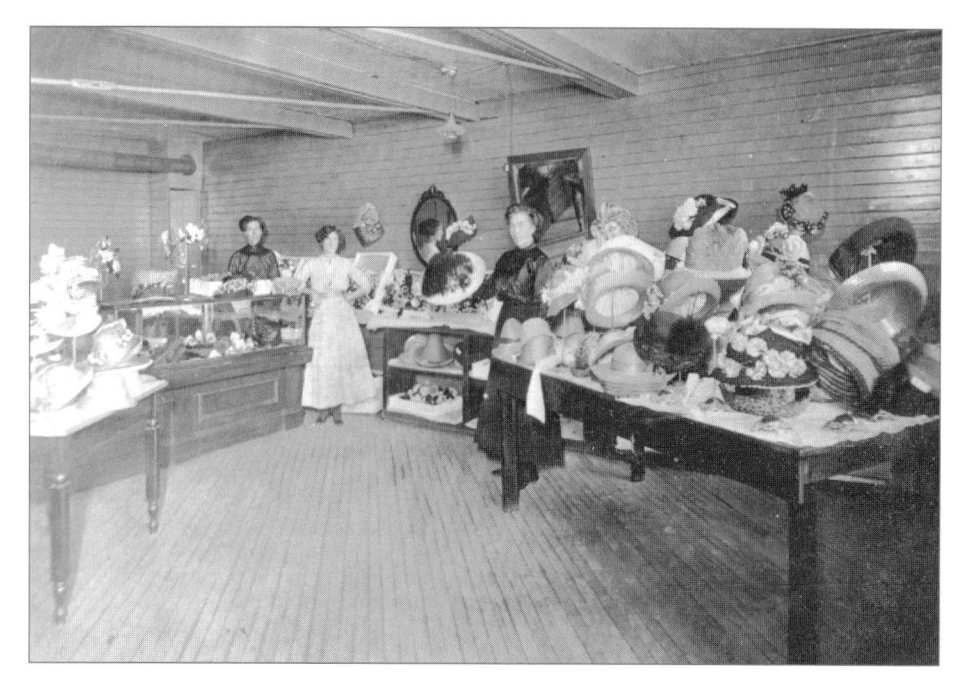

A number of buildings or building sites in Cloquet have served multiple roles. The millinery shop shown here in 1918, was located on the south side of Cloquet Avenue between Ninth and Tenth streets on the site later occupied by the Tulip Shoppe. Notice how the assortment of hats and other finery contrast with the rather crude construction of the building. The long horizontal chimney pipe leading to a half chimney, the open electrical wiring in the background, and the tie rods and turnbuckles spanning the ceiling indicate the structure was probably built in haste.

John Antioho, proprietor of the Tulip Shoppe, is shown behind the counter of his ice cream parlor, restaurant, and Greyhound Bus stop. Notice the elaborately carved classic soda fountain and mirror in the background. Such masterpieces of Victorian art rivaled any saloon decor of the time. The early fountains were often self-contained. They included their own gas generators which were used to produce carbonated beverages in the days before soda was sold in bottles. John's shop was a gathering place for many generations of high school students, as well as a point of departure and arrival for bus passengers.

Specialty stores, such as meat markets, have always enjoyed a measure of success in Cloquet. Grunig's Meat Market was a well-patronized store. The three unidentified men standing in the entrance may be the store's proprietors. The horse and delivery wagon stand ready to deliver the next load of groceries to some homemaker.

B&B Market, owned by Kim and John Lind and located at 509 Pleasant Avenue, is the successor of many early neighborhood stores that once existed in Cloquet. Today this modern marketplace features not only catering service, but also is noted for its quality meats.

Photo by Timothy J. Krohn

One frequent destination for shoppers was Cloquet's Southgate Shopping Center, shown in this 1976 photograph. It is an interesting fact that many shopping centers are named "gate," even when no "gate" is present. The term "dale" was formerly associated with shopping centers in large metropolitan areas, but the term gate began to emerge in the 1970s, about the same time the political scandal associated with the Watergate Hotel in Washington D.C. was uncovered. Just exactly what the connection is between a shopping center and a hotel is not clear.

133

In recent decades large grocery stores, such as Super One, have located in Cloquet. Characterized by a large assortment of brand name products, such stores can frequently offer competitive prices based on large volume purchases. In this photograph store employee, Chuck Strand, is busy checking the shelves.

Photo by Timothy J. Krohn

The latest addition to the list of large marketplaces in Cloquet is the new Wal-Mart Super Center. This new store seems far removed from the early specialty markets with their horse drawn delivery wagons, yet the change took place in a relatively short time.

Photo by Timothy J. Krohn

Although Cloquet is not often thought of as a tourist destination, that perception is rapidly changing. Facilities such as the Cloquet Area Recreation Center and well-groomed snowmobile trails draw many visitors for hockey tournaments and other outdoor recreational activities.

Photo by Timothy J. Krohn

One of the latest attractions in the Cloquet area is the new Black Bear Casino and Hotel Complex owned by the Fond du Lac Indian Reservation. Where once the wood industries of Cloquet were the leading employer in the community, they have since been surpassed. The Reservation is now the largest single employer in the entire county. It is also interesting to note that this latest addition to the Reservation's businesses is located at another important crossroads just south of Cloquet.

The new 18-hole championship Black Bear Golf Course is located next to the Black Bear Casino and Hotel complex. Shown here is Hole Number 11.

Photos by Rocky Wilkinson courtesy of the Fond du Lac Reservation

This 2003 aerial view shows present-day Cloquet looking east. The smokestacks of the Sappi Fine Paper Co. can be seen in the upper center of the photo. The new Highway 33 bridge spans the St. Louis River and the Spafford Park campground can be seen on the river bank in the lower left.

Photo by Timothy J. Krohn

Walter O'Meara was a well-known author who grew up in Cloquet during the early years of the twentieth century. In addition to his many published works of history and fiction, O'Meara is remembered by some as the author of the lyrics of the Cloquet High School song. His memorable story of growing up in Cloquet, *We Made It Through the Winter: A Memoir of Northern Minnesota Boyhood*, told of his early years here. His life spanned many of the years covered by this volume and his work set the standard by which all future authors wishing to describe Cloquet will be measured.

A Color Album

Clockwise from top-center ~

Catholic Church
Swedish Lutheran Church & Parsonage
Northwest Paper Mill
Water Power Mill
Northern Lumber Company Planer
Presbyterian Church & Parsonage
Public Library
Johnson-Wentworth Company Mill
High School
Arch Street

Postcard from before the 1918 Fire.

Ever since the public announcement in 1839 of the first photographic processes, photographers have sought ways to add color to their images. Since the early days of photography, colors have been added to photos with colored dyes, oil paints, and pencils. In the early 1900s, many of these hand-colored photos were printed as postcards. Postcards became a fast, inexpensive method of communication and have been popular ever since. After the introduction of Kodachrome film in 1935 and Kodacolor roll film in 1941, photographers began taking photos in color. This "color album" provides examples of a number of the color processes used to record history throughout Cloquet's last 100 years.

Log jam at Cloquet

Postcard c. early 1900s

Cloquet Public Library and Post Office. The Shaw Memorial Library was built after the fire with funds from insurance and donations by the daughters of George S. Shaw, an early lumberman. It was used as a library until 1987 when it became the home of the Carlton County Historical Society.

The Northwest Paper Company mill was constructed beginning in 1898 with numerous additions through the years. The mill survived the fire and played an important role in reviving the economy of Cloquet.

The Berst Company began making clothespins, tongue depressors and matches in 1905. The company later became Berst-Forster-Dixfield and then Diamond Match Co.

Postcards, c. late 1930s

The country's only Frank Lloyd Wright designed gas station is located at the corner of Highways 33 and 45. It was built in 1958 and features a cantilevered canopy which projects 32 feet over the gas pumps.

The Cloquet Community Memorial Hospital opened in August, 1958 in the Sunnyside area overlooking the St. Louis River. A 42 bed Convalescent and Nursing Care unit was completed in March, 1965. Another addition is being built and is scheduled to open in 2004.

Postcards, c. late 1960s

Engine #16 of the Duluth and Northeastern Railroad makes one of its last trips before being retired in 1964 to Fauley Park. It was built in 1913 by the Baldwin Locomotive Works and now belongs to the city of Cloquet. The photo was taken April, 1963.

Enid, Vickey, and Gerry Whittenberg are ready for winter fun in this hand-colored photo from 1932.

Bob, John, Viana, Irene, and Lempi Laaksonen pose for the camera c. 1920s.

Cloquet High School band members, Gerard Antus, John Poferl, and Jack Pigman are ready to march in this photo taken about 1942.

Hand- coloring photos such as these was an enjoyable hobby for many amateur photographers.

140

Do You Remember When...

...the Chief Theater showed Clint Eastwood films? The building at 103 Avenue C has been renovated and now houses Antiques Off Broadway. Photo, 1969

...all the fire hydrants in town were decorated for the Bicentennial of 1976?

Photo by Dan Unulock.

...the band shell in Pinehurst Park was painted with this bright colored mural?

It is pictured here after a large storm damaged trees around 1985.

Photo courtesy of Harriette Niemi.

...employees of Northwest Paper and later Potlatch received a pad of paper with a Mountie print cover with every paycheck?

Used with permission of Tweed Museum of Art, University of Minnesota Duluth.

Parades have always been an important part of Cloquet's 4th of July and Labor Day celebrations.

No parade would be complete without marching bands, politicians, and floats.

Top and middle right photos by Milo Rasmussen
Middle left photo by Harold Olson

142

A TALE of TWO TOWERS

The old water tower was a beloved landmark and symbol of courage for those who came back and rebuilt Cloquet after the fires of 1918.

Photo by Timothy J. Krohn, 2003

Photo by Marlene Wisuri

The new water tower was under construction in the fall of 2002.

Photo by Phil E. Larson

The new water tower peeks above the trees behind the home built by Frederick Weyerhaeuser after the fire. It later became the Potlatch Staff House and is now privately owned. It is part of the Park Place Historic District which was named to the National Registry of Historic Places in 1985.

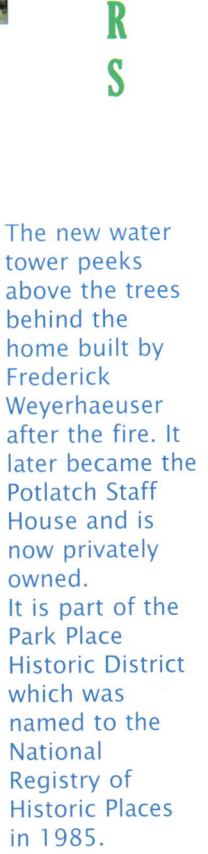

Photo by Timothy J. Krohn

Gordy's Hi-Hat has been a favorite spot to "grab a burger" for residents and visitors alike since its opening in 1960. These travelers stopped by in 1969.

Cloquet Transit Company is one of the older businesses in Cloquet.
The company currently maintains a fleet of modern charter and school buses.

The Hotel Solem and Cloquet Avenue in the 1950s. The Solem was opened by A. J. Solem in 1919 and an addition was completed in 1923.

This collection of photos of the West End businesses on Avenue C was taken in 1969 by Ray Riihiluoma.

City employees Barb Wayman, Jim Prusak, Bill Schlenvogt, and Brian Fritsinger pose in front of the new city hall.

Cloquet has a paid fire department with 20 firefighters. Steve Hills, Sean Saddler, Chief Jim Langenbrunner, John Hecht, and Kevin Toboleski are pictured, left to right, in front of five of the department's fire trucks and two emergency vehicles.

Photos by Timothy J. Krohn

The President and Board of Directors of the Cloquet/Carlton County Area Chamber of Commerce are pictured in front of the chamber offices, built in 1995-96 and located on Highway 33 in the Sunnyside area.

Photos by Timothy J. Krohn.

Dr. Don Day was inaugurated as the second President of Fond du Lac Tribal and Community College in 2003. The college is the only tribal/state co-governed community college in the country and has seen great growth in numbers of students since its beginnings in Garfield School under the leadership of the late Lester "Jack" Briggs in 1987.

The striking architecture of the FDLTCC glows in this night photo by Jonathan Chapman.

The Cloquet High School Madrigal Singers gathered on the steps of the Carlton County History & Heritage Center on November 23, 1996. Their performance was part of the Downtown Merchants' holiday celebration following the completion of improvements to Cloquet Avenue.

After an absence of many years, the Cloquet Community Band was reorganized in 1998. The Band performs a number of concerts every year and is pictured here on July 4, 2003. They will participate in Cloquet's Centennial Celebration in 2004.

Photo courtesy of Carol Risdon

While it is no longer possible to "catch a flick" at the LEB or the CHIEF theaters, Premiere Theatres offers current feature films in a multi-plex setting located on Highway 33. Pictured in 2003 are theater employees Karen Brungardt, Cary Neumann, and Tyler Korby.

Photo by Timothy J. Krohn

Bergquist Imports has provided Scandinavian gifts to a local and nationwide clientele since its founding in 1948. Vivian and Barry Bergquist cut-up with the cut-outs in front of the retail store on Hwy 33.

Photo by Timothy J. Krohn, 2003

NHL hockey star and Cloquet High School graduate, Jamie Langenbrunner, brought the Stanley Cup to Cloquet for the second time in 2003.

Photo by Mike Sylvester, *Pine Journal*, 2003

Cloquet has been served by local newspapers since the 1880s. In 2002 the long-published *Pine Knot* merged with the *Cloquet Journal* to become the *Pine Journal*. Joel Soukkala, Jill Beyer, Kathryn Cota, Julie Schultz, and editor, Wendy Johnson are pictured in front of the office at 813 Cloquet Avenue.

Photo by Timothy J. Krohn, 2003.

The Sappi Fine Paper mill.

Cloquet at Night

Photos by Timothy J. Krohn

Winter, 2003-2004

Looking east on Avenue C in the west end.

Cloquet Avenue looking west.

The Little Store on Hwy 33 and Broadway with the old water tower seen on the hill behind.

Centennial Activities

Artist Fleta Carroll, paints *Railway Through the Past* which is one of the murals in the Centennial's outdoor mural project. It is located at 11th Street and Cloquet Avenue and depicts a logging train in winter.

The first of Cloquet's Historic Markers was dedicated on October, 13, 2003, in Fauley Park. It tells the story of early Cloquet and the 1918 Fire.

Photos by Marlene Wisuri

A rendezvous reinactment was held in July, 2003, on Dunlap Island as a "trial run" for the Centennial celebration of 2004.

Photo by Timothy J. Krohn

151

View of the city looking east taken from the old water tower in the summer of 2003.

Photo by Timothy J. Krohn

The St. Louis River and the west end with the bridge to Dunlap Island, USG on the left, and the Northeastern on the right. Summer, 2003.

Photo by Allen Anway

Bibliography

The following works were consulted in the preparation of this book. They consist mainly of published materials and cover a broad spectrum of subjects pertaining to Cloquet's history. Additional resources, covering more specific topics, can be found in the bibliographies of many of the works listed below or in the collections of the Carlton County Historical Society.

Beck, Bill. *Northern Lights: An Illustrated History of Minnesota Power.* Duluth, 1986.

Carroll, Francis M. *Crossroads in Time: A History of Carlton County, Minnesota.* Cloquet, 1987.

Carroll, Francis M. and Franklin R. Raiter. *The Fires of Autumn: The Cloquet-Moose Lake Disaster of 1918.* St. Paul, 1990.

_____. "The People Versus the Government: The 1918 Cloquet Fire and the Struggle for Compensation." *Journal of Forest History.* vol. 29 (January, 1985).

_____. " 'At the Time of our Misfortune:' Relief Efforts Following the 1918 Cloquet Fire." *Minnesota History.* vol. 48 (Fall, 1983).

Carroll, Francis M. and Marlene Wisuri. *Reflections of Our Past: A Pictorial History of Carlton County, Minnesota.* Cloquet, 1997.

Cloquet: Home of the White Pine. Moose Lake, 1978 [First published in 1907].

Cloquet, Minnesota: An Industrial Study of Cloquet—The City That Really Came Back. N.p., c. 1930.

Coleman, Sister Bernard. *Where the Water Stops: Fond du Lac Reservation.* Duluth, 1967.

Fahlstrom, Paul Gerin. *Old Cloquet: White Pine Capital of the World.* Baltimore, 1997.

_____. *Anna Dickie and Peter Olesen, Notable Citizens of Cloquet.* Cloquet, 1996.

Gray, Kathryn Elfes. "50 Years of Progress Since 1918 Holocaust." *The Pine Knot.* October 10, 1968.

_____. "William Kelly—Cloquet's First Merchant." *Cloquet Vidette.* August 16, 1967.

Harrison, Frederick G. *Cinders and Timber: A Bird's-eye View of Logging Railroads in Northeastern Minnesota Yesterday and Today.* N.p., 1967.

Hemingson, Ray E. *Death by Fire: The Story of the Great Northeastern Minnesota Forest Fire.* Waupaca, 1985.

Hindy, Ralph W., Frank Ernest Hill and Allan Nevins. *Timber and Men: The Weyerhaeuser Story.* New York, 1963.

Holbrook, Stewart H. *Burning an Empire: The Story of American Forest Fires.* New York, 1943.

King, Frank A. *Minnesota Logging Railroads.* San Marino, 1981.

Larson, Agnes M. *History of the White Pine in Minnesota.* Minneapolis, 1945.

Luukkonen, Arnold L. "Brave Men in Their Motor Machines--and the 1918 Forest Fire." *Ramsey County History.* Fall, 1972.

Luukkonen, Larry. "Return to Fortress Island, Landmark in the St. Louis." *The Pine Knot.* July 8, 1995.

_____. "Memories of the Fire: Some Family Experiences During the Fire of 1918." *Remembering the Fires of 1918—80 Years Later.* [Unpublished manuscript prepared for the Carlton County Historical Society] Cloquet, 1998.

_____. "Portages and Posés on the St. Louis River," in "Tales of the Old Northwest Trail." *Aitkin Independent Age.* December 1, 1999.

_____. *Cloquet: The Story Behind the Name.* Cloquet, 2000.

_____. "The Fire Bear: A Symbol of Survival." *Aitkin Independent Age.* October 26, 2001 [Reprinted in *The Pine Knot.* March 20, 2002].

_____. "Forgotten Pathway of the Voyageurs," in "Tales of the Old Northwest Trail." *Aitkin Independent Age.* March 7, 2001.

Niemi, Harriette. "Awfullest Fire Horror in State's History." Cloquet, 1976.

Niemi, Harriette and Mike Knievel, "Cloquet Public Library." *The Pine Knot.* June 28, 1979.

O'Meara, Walter. *The Trees Went Forth.* New York, 1947.

_____. *We Made it Through the Winter: A Memoir of Northern Minnesota Boyhood.* St. Paul, 1974.

Peacock, Thomas D.(ed.). *A Forever Story: The People and Community of the Fond du Lac Reservation.* Cloquet, 1998.

Pelkonen, Matt. "Cloquet on Parade." Carlton County Historical Society (CCHS) Files, n.d.

Ryan, J. C. *Early Loggers in Minnesota.* 4 vols. Duluth, 1973-84.

Schantz-Hanson, Dr. T. "Cloquet and the Forest Industries." CCHS Files, n.d.

_____. "The History of the Cloquet School District." CCHS Files, n.d.

Skalko, Christine and Marlene Wisuri, *Fire Storm: The Great Fires of 1918.* Cloquet, 2003.

Sommer, Barbara. "The City That Really Came Back," *Cloquet and the Fire of 1918.* Cloquet, 1985.

The Fury of the Flames: A Pictorial History of the Great Forest Fires of Northern Minnesota October 12-15, 1918. Cloquet, Moose Lake, 1998.

Thorpe, Dr. James. *Carlton County History.* 6 vols. [Unpublished manuscript prepared for the Carlton County Historical Society] Cloquet, n.d.

_____."History" [Scrapbook of articles prepared for the Carlton County Historical Society] Cloquet, n.d.

Watkins, Mrs. C. B. (ed.) "A Group of Essays Written by Cloquet Fire Sufferers." CCHS Files, 1936.

Suggested Readings

There have been a number of books published about Cloquet and Carlton County. Here is a list of some of the titles that are available for purchase at the Carlton County History & Heritage Center Store. Many of them can also be borrowed from libraries.

Beck, Bennett A. *Brief History of the Pioneers of the Cromwell, Minnesota Area*, Carlton County Historical Society, Cloquet, MN. 2001.

Carroll, Francis M. *Crossroads in Time: A History of Carlton County, Minnesota*. Carlton County Historical Society, Cloquet, MN. 1987.

Carroll, Francis M. and Franklin R. Raiter. *The Fires of Autumn: The Cloquet-Moose Lake Disaster of 1918*. Minnesota Historical Society Press, St. Paul, MN. 1990.

Carroll, Francis M. and Marlene Wisuri. *Reflections of Our Past: A Pictorial History of Carlton County, Minnesota*. Donning Company, Virginia Beach, VA. 1997.

Fahlstrom, Paul. *Anna Dickie and Peter Olesen: Notable Citizens of Cloquet*. Carlton County Historical Society, Cloquet, MN. 1996.

Fahlstrom, Paul. *Old Cloquet, Minnesota – White Pine Capitol of the World*, Gateway Press, Inc. Balitmore, MD. 1997.

1918 Fire Stories. Moose Lake Area Historical Society, Moose Lake, MN. 2003.

Luukkonen, Larry. *Cloquet: The Story Behind the Name*. Carlton County Historical Society, Cloquet, MN. 2000.

Mattinen, John A. translated by Richard Impola, *History of the Thomson Farming Area*, Carlton County Historical Society, Cloquet, MN. 2000.

O'Meara, Walter. *We Made It Through the Winter: A Memoir of Northern Minnesota Boyhood*. Minnesota Historical Society Press, St. Paul, MN. 1974.

Peacock, Thomas D. (ed.) *A Forever Story: The People and Community of the Fond du Lac Reservation*. Fond du Lac Band of Lake Superior Chippewa, Cloquet, MN. 1998.

Skalko, Christine and Marlene Wisuri. *Fire Storm: The Great Fires of 1918*, Carlton County Historical Society, Cloquet, MN. 2003.

Index

Anderson, Carl L., 100
Anderson, Frank, 58
Anderson, Fritz, 28
Antioho, John, 132
Antiques Off Broadway, 141
Antus, Gerard, 140
Arch Street, 20, 28, 32, 137
American Fur Company, 17, 36
Anakkala, Alex, 87
B & B Market, 133
Balsam-Wool, 121, 127, 128
Baumann-Nesthus Men's Store, 129
Belfry, Scott, 116
Berg, Harry, 96
Berg, Morrie, 96
Bergeron, John, 42
Bergeron, Lawrence, 86
Bergquist, Barry, 149
Bergquist Imports, 149
Bergquist, Vivian, 149
Berst-Forster-Dixfield Company, 40, 120, 121, 138
Beyer, Jill, 149
Big Lake, 72
Bijou Theater, 63
Black Bear Casino and Hotel, 135
Black Bear Golf Course, 135
Blinn, Ned, 94
Boldt, Oscar J. Construction, 123
Bonneville, Albert, 94
Boquist, Elizabeth, 58
Botner, Ardis, 59
Bourdeau, Don, 59
Boy Scout Troup 174, 51
Boyer, William, 87
Brandenburg, Henry, 38
Brekke, Esther, 59
Bridgeman's, 34
Briggs, Lester "Jack," 147
Brooks-Scanlon Lumber Company, 41
Brungardt, Karen, 148
Bushey, Shirley, 59
Buskala, Emil, 94
Buskala, Joanne, 130
Buskala, John, 130
Buskala's Jewelry Store, 130
Cameron, Daniel, 37, 40

Camp Coy, 72
Campbell, Camilla, 92
Campbell, Winifred, 92
Canfield, Tom, 52
Cardinal, Lawrence, 112
Carl Anderson American Legion Post, 110, 116
Carlson, Henfen, 94
Carlson, Julius, 94
Carlton, 18
Carlton County Historical Society, 63, 138
Carlton County History & Heritage Center, 148
Carroll, Fleta, 151
Caza, Joseph, 131
Centennial activities, 151
Chief Theater, 63, 141, 148
Childs, Frances O'Meara, 91
Chounard, E., 127
Christenson, Jim, 52
Churchill Elementary School, 59
Church of the Holy Names of Jesus and Mary, 56, 137
Civilian Conservation Corps (CCC), 111
Clark, Lester, 86
Cloquet Area Recreation Center, 134
Cloquet Athletic Club, 93
Cloquet Auto & Supply Company, 31, 106
Cloquet Avenue, 32
Cloquet Baseball Team, 94
Cloquet Boarding House, 80
Cloquet Box Company, 40,
Cloquet-Carlton County Area Chamber of Commerce, 147
Cloquet City Band, 68
Cloquet City Halls, 33, 146
Cloquet Commercial Club, 72
Cloquet Community Band, 148
Cloquet Co-op Bowling Team, 92
Cloquet Cooperative Society, 66, 75, 78, 80, 113
Cloquet-Duluth Transit Company, 30
Cloquet Fire Department, 52, 83, 86, 146

Cloquet Forest Experimental Station, 5, 48, 71
Cloquet Gymnastic Team, 67
Cloquet High School, 61, 93, 95, 97, 137
Cloquet High School Band, 64, 140
Cloquet High School Madrigal Singers, 148
Cloquet Independent, 74
Cloquet Journal, 149
Cloquet Labor Temple, 65, 73
Cloquet Lumber Company, 27, 38, 39, 42, 44, 90
Cloquet Lumber Company's Big Store, 74
Cloquet Post Office, 111, 138
Cloquet Public Library, 62, 137, 138
Cloquet River, 16
Cloquet Theater, 63
Cloquet Tie and Post Company, 39
Cloquet Transit Company, 144
Cloquet Valley Ranger Station, 49
Cloquet Water Line, 85
Cloquet Water Tower, 85, 143
Community Memorial Hospital, 82, 139
Conner, Joe, 92
Copeland, Stuart, 52
Cota, Kathryn, 149
Coy, Edward D., 52
Coy, Elizabeth, 52
Crider, Charles, 40
Crider, Wayne, 96
Crotty, Thomas J., 126
Daigle, Theodore, 127
Daughters of Norway, 46, 64
Davis, Kathryn, 92
Day, Don, 147
Dean, Joseph, 127
Demers, Harry, 127
Diamond Match Company, 40, 120, 138
Diamond Theater, 63
Dobrowolski, Arthur C., 112
Dolan, Maxine, 92

Dormanen, Mary, 47
Drew, Herb, 95
Driscoll, Margaret, 92
Duluth & Northeastern Railroad (D & NE), 26, 27, 108, 118, 125, 139
Dunlap Island, 20, 22, 26, 38, 81, 82, 84, 108, 152
Dupont, William H., 115
Erickson, Elsie, 59
Evans, Lynette, 58
Fauley Park, 71, 139, 151
Finnish Athletic Association, 94
Finnish Brass Band, 68
Finnish Temperance Society, 66
Finnish Workers' Hall, 73
Fire of 1918, 33, 48, 62, 67, 94, 102-107, 111, 151
Fond du Lac, 17
Fond du Lac Tribal & Community College, 62, 147
Fond du Lac Reservation, 16, 36, 103, 117, 123, 135
Forslund, Agnes M., 58
Fortress Island, 14, 15
Franklin, Clarabelle, 126
Freeman Hotel, 81
Fritsinger, Brian, 146
Frost, O. W., 127
G & W Refrigerator Company, 129
Garfield School, 51, 58
Gaskill, Al, 94
Gellerman, Henry H., 88
General Light and Power Company, 121, 122
Genin, Rev. John B., 21
Godfrey, Francis J. "Cheech," 114
Golen, Charles, 96
Golen, Dave, 96
Golden, Gail, 58
Golden, Terry, 58
Gordy's Hi-Hat, 144
Grand Theater, 63
Great Depression, 106, 111
Great Northern Railroad, 26
Graves, C. H., 38
Grunig's farm, 77
Grunig's Meat Market, 133
Hagen, Hannah, 91
Hall, Gloria, 50
Harwood, William D., 38
Hauptmann, William, 86
Hawkinson, Swan, 41
Hebert Taxi, 30
Hebert, Walter E. "Spec," 30

Hecht, John, 146
Hills, Steve, 146
Historic Markers, 151
Hoffren, Axel, 68
Holy Family Mission, 21, 55
Hornby, Henry C., 44
Hubert, Herbert J., 96
Huot, Estelle & Oliver, 47, 122
Huot, LeBeau, 122
Husby, Gunelle, 92
Jaycee Women, 72
Jefferson School, 48, 59
Jenkins, A. F., 127
Jenkins, Dave, 52
Johnson, Arthur L., 99
Johnson, Helen, 58
Johnson, Marion Jesse, 91
Johnson Mercantile Company, 109
Johnson, Nelly Everson, 69
Johnson, Samuel S., 39
Johnson, "Snowball," 69
Johnson, Wendy, 149
Johnson-Wentworth Company, 39, 42, 44, 137
Jurek, Anthony F., 116
Kalbrener, Gretchen, 58
Kalbrener, Tom, 58
Kaner, Elsie, 92
Kaner, Harry, 50, 87
Kaner, Rose, 59
Kelly, Leone, 92
Kenety, Ava, 92
Kenety, Kathleen, 92
Killpu, Matt, 69
Klippen Scandinavian Lodge #3, 54
Knife Falls, 12, 15, 16, 17, 18, 35, 122, 124
Knife Falls Boom Company, 18, 38
Knife Falls Dam, 23
Knife Falls Lumber Company, 38, 39
Knife Portage, 14, 16, 17
Knife Falls Township, 17, 20, 23,
Kolseth & Anderson, 79
Korby, Tyler, 148
Kronemann, Don, 60
L & M Supply, 123
Laaksonen, Bob, 140
Laaksonen, Irene, 140
Laaksonen, John, 140
Laaksonen, Lempi, 140
Laaksonen, Mae, 131
Laaksonen, Viana, 140
Ladies of Kaleva, 65
Lake Superior, 15
Lake Superior & Mississippi Railroad, 36

Lange, Jessica, 50
Langenbrunner, Jamie, 149
Langenbrunner, Jim, 146
Larson, Jalmar M., 127
Larson, Leonard R., 127
Larson, Myron, 127
LaTulip, Tony, 83
LaVoi, Helen, 91
Leach, L. F., 44
Leach School, 48, 60, 70
LEB Theater, 63, 69, 148
Lehne, Otto, 102
Leonard, Paul, 94
Lind, Carl, 79
Lind, John, 133
Lind, Kim, 133
Lindquist, Eric, 68
Little Store, 150
Loisel, Simore, 94
Loyal Order of Moose, 64
Luke, Ray, 130
Lumppio, Alfred, 68
Lund, Ivar, 127
Lund, Karen, 59
Lundblad, Evelyn, 59
Luukkonen, Arnold M., 86, 113
Luukkonen, Emil, 68
Luukkonen, Larry, 113
Maki, George, 52
Manley, Dale, 52
Marshall, G. E., 48
Martinson, Joan, 59
Masonic Lodge, 64
Maynard, Charles, 127
Mayors of Cloquet, 8
McKale, A., 40
McCoy and Sapp's Garage, 29
McKenna, Evelyn, 94
McKinnon House, 80
McNair, C. I., 39, 126
McNair, Ruth, 92
McNair, William K., 38, 44
McSweeney, John, 87
Milepost 62, 103
Minnesota Home Guard, 105
Minogue, Bob, 96
Monroe, Ed, 45
Montreal Hotel, 81
Moorhead Road, 20
Moose Saloon, 81, 131
Morneau, Octavie, 36
Musser, Drew, 39
Nahgahnub (Nagonub), Joseph, 35
Nelson, Charles N., 38
Nelson, Edwin C., 87
Nelson, Ellen, 59

Nelson Opera House, 63
Nelson, J. William, 127
Neuman, Cary, 148
Newman, Frank, 40
Nicollet, Joseph N., 15, 16
Nick's Cavaliers, 69
Noble, Chuck, 52
Norman, August & Annie, 47
Norman, Edith, 92
Norquist, Harry, 87
Northeastern Hotel, 81, 82, 152
Northern Lumber Company, 6, 25, 27, 41, 43, 103, 105, 108, 118, 137
Northern Lumber Company Boarding House, 80
Northern Pacific Junction, 18
Northern Pacific Railroad, 19
Northwest Company, 36
Northwest Paper Company, 43, 93, 112, 115, 120, 121, 122, 125, 126, 137, 138, 141
Norwegian Lutheran Church, 56
Nu-Wood, 121, 127
Odegaard, Velma, 59
O'Donnell House, 80
O'Meara, Walter, 136
Olesen, Anna Dickie, 48
Olesen, Peter, 48
Olds, Sheldon H., 38
Olin, Ruth, 92
Olsen, Herman, 130
Olsen Shoe Shop, 130
Olson, Olaf, 36
Order of the Eastern Star, 64
Order of Foresters, 64
Oswald House, 80
Our Lady of the Sacred Heart Church, 46, 56
Paine, James M., 38
Park Place Historic District, 143
Pastika, Joseph, 87
Peck, Gregory, 50
Peterson, Margaret Ann, 59
Petite, Mr. & Mrs. Joe, 19
Peyton, Barbara, 50
Pinehurst Park, 21, 83, 84, 90, 91, 115, 141
Pine Journal, 149
Pine Knot, 74, 109, 149
Poirer, Ray, 86
Perrault, Jean Bapitste, 35
Pigman, Jack, 140
Pleinis, Teresa Smith, 117
Poferl, John, 140
Pollak, Nathan, 117
Posey Island, 19, 25

Posey, Joe, 19
Premiere Theatres, 148
Presbyterian Church of Cloquet, 57, 137
Prusak, Jim, 146
Puumala, Barbara Meyer, 49
Puumala, Marie Bepko, 49
Puumala, Reino H., 49
Puumala, Ricard, 49, 113
Queen of Peace Parish, 46
Queen of Peace School, 58
Rahiikinen, Arvid, 68
Randall, Mike, 96
Rathbone-Hair-Ridgway Company, 40, 124
Rautio, Art, 130
Reed, Adolph, 127
Reed, E., 127
Renwick, Shaw & Crosset, 44
Reponen, Einar, 94
Riihiluoma, Ray Inc., 123
Ridlington, Daniel S., 127
Ridlington, Robert W., 127
Rogentine, Toge, 94
Rosted, Ruth, 59
Rotary Club, 64, 71
Royal Neighbors, 64
Rud, Sylvia, 59
Ryan, J. C. "Buzz," 49
Sabin, Dwight M., 38
Saddler, Sean, 146
Sage, Rev., 58
St. Andrew's Episcopal Church, 57, 58
St. Casimir's Church, 46, 57
St. Louis River, 12, 14, 15, 17, 19, 20, 22, 23, 35, 42, 55, 84, 108, 111, 119, 121, 122, 136, 152
St. Paul and Duluth Railroad, 18, 22, 38
St. Paul's Academy, 58
St. Paul's Church, 57
Sahlman, George, 102
Sandstrom, Dr. Carl, 94
Sandstrom, Madge, 92
Sappi Fine Paper, 120, 136, 150
Saturday Musicale, 63
Sawmill Days, 53
Schantz-Hanson, T., 48
Scheibe, Clarence, 87
Schlenvogt, Bill, 146
Schultz, Julie, 149
Shaw, George S., 39, 43
Shaw Memorial Library, 62, 88
Siltanen, Aili, 59
Smith, James, Jr., 38
Smith, Mike & Maggie, 47

Solem, A. J., 145
Solem Hotel, 81, 145
Sons of Norway, 64
Soukkala, Joel, 149
Southgate Shopping Center, 133
Spafford Park, 136
Spafford, Virginia, 92
Spanish Influenza, 105
Stanley Cup, 149
Streator, E. S., 127
Super One, 134
Swanson, Bruce, 52
Swedish Lutheran Church, 137
Syralia (Syrjälä), Bill, 68, 69
Trainer Aircraft Company, 129
Toboleski, Kevin, 146
Toivola Company, 80, 102
Trevors, Mr., 130
Tufflex, 128
Tulip Shoppe, 132
Tuominen, Francis W., 47
Upper Lakes Foods, 123
U. S. Gypsum (USG), 123, 152
Vibert, Percy, 40
Viking Male Chorus, 64, 70
WKLK Radio, 73
Walker, Kenneth, 86
Wal-Mart Super Center, 123, 134
Walter, Lynn, 58
Ward, Marion, 92
Washington School, 60
Water Power Company, 38, 39, 121, 137
Wayman, Barb, 146
Wentworth Square, 13
Weyerhaeuser, Charles, 39
Weyerhaeuser, Frederick, 39, 42, 143
Weyerhaeuser, Frederick E., 39
Weyerhaeuser, Rudolph, 39, 42
Whittenberg, Enid, 140
Whittenberg, Gerry, 140
Whittenberg, Vickey, 140
Wilson, Sylvester "Stokes," 8
Women's Friday Club, 62
Wood Conversion Company, 41, 110, 118, 120, 121, 127, 128
World War I, 94, 98, 99, 100-102
World War II, 20, 106, 112-115
Wright Apartments, 131
Wright, Frank Lloyd, 139
YMCA, 64, 67
Yanda, Beatrice, 114
Yetka, Lawrence, 49

About the Authors

Larry Luukkonen was born and raised in Cloquet. He attended the University of Minnesota, where he received his Bachelor of Science, Master of Arts, and was admitted to candidacy for the Ph.D. all in history. He taught in his chosen field at the University of Minnesota, Bemidji State University, and in the Minnesota Community College system. He has written several scholarly works including *Terms of the Trade: Some Words and Expressions Used in the Fur Trade* and *Cloquet: The Story Behind The Name*. He has also written over fifty magazine and newspaper feature articles, all dealing with various aspects of early Minnesota History. He is a frequent guest lecturer and has appeared on public television and radio. He has also served as a consultant for museums and video productions dealing with the history of Northern Minnesota.

Marlene Wisuri has served as the director of the Carlton County Historical Society since 1992. She has co-authored several books including *Reflections of Our Past: A Pictorial History of Carlton County* with Francis Carroll, *Ojibwe: Waasa Inaabidaa – We Look in All Directions* with Thomas Peacock, and *Fire Storm: The Great Fires of 1918* with Christine Skalko. She has taught photography and photo history at several colleges and universities and her photographic work has been widely exhibited regionally, nationally, and in Finland and Norway. Her undergraduate work was done at the College of St. Scholastica and she holds a Master of Fine Arts degree from the University of Massachusetts-Dartmouth.

Author photos by Kathyrn Nordstrom, Studio One